Spreading
the Word

John Aitchison, Professor Emeritus at the University of Wales, Aberystwyth, joined the staff of the Department of Geography (as it then was) in 1967. He was subsequently appointed to the endowed Gregynog Chair of Human Geography in 1989. For two years he also held research fellowships at the Institut de Géographie, Sorbonne in Paris. At Aberystwyth he established the Rural Surveys Research Unit (an applied research consultancy), and co-founded the highly-regarded International Centre for Protected Landscapes. For his pioneer work on the 'Common Lands of Wales' he received a Prince of Wales Award. In addition to his extensive research on the Welsh language, he has written widely on matters relating to rural and environmental issues in England and Wales, and, under contract to various French Government Ministries and the European Commission, on socio-economic change in rural France.

Harold Carter, Professor Emeritus at the University of Wales, Aberystwyth, held the Gregynog Chair of Human Geography between 1968 and 1986 and was Head of Department (1983-6) and Vice-Principal (1981-3). During his career he was Visiting Professor and subsequently Distinguished Visiting Professor at the University of Cincinnati, Lefrak Lecturer and Visiting Professor at the University of Maryland, Visiting Professor at the Unuiversity of Stellenbosch and British Council Distinguished University Scholar in Australia. He was President of the Institute of British Geographers in 1986. His text books on urban geography came to be standard works of reference and were translated into several languages. For his writings on the geography of Wales, including its language and culture, he was made a member of the Gorsedd of Bards at the Llanrwst Eisteddfod in 1990.

John Aitchison & Harold Carter

Spreading the Word

THE WELSH LANGUAGE 2001

ENOUGH IS ENOUGH
DEMANDING
WELSH EDUCATION

YN PARHAU I FRWYDRO!
ADDYSG GYMRAEG DEREC!

y Lolfa

Cover photograph by Arvid Parry-Jones shows tudents at the
University of Wales, Aberystwyth demonstrating for an
increased provision of teaching through the medium of Welsh
(February, 2004)

ISBN: 0 86243 714 8

Printed and published in Wales
by Y Lolfa Cyf., Talybont, Ceredigion SY24 5AP
e-mail ylolfa@ylolfa.com
website www.ylolfa.com
tel. (01970) 832 304
fax 832 782

are derived – 'Can you understand, speak, read or write Welsh?'. Phrased in this way the question can be answered on very different bases, and at a variety of different levels. This is partly because no attempt is made to differentiate degrees of fluency in the language. To cite but one complication, it seems highly likely that in completing the census schedule many parents of children who attend Welsh lessons at school will have been tempted to answer 'yes' on their behalf, whereas their ability to communicate in the language might in fact have been limited to a few rudimentary sentences. But all questionnaires have their weaknesses and little more can be done about it other than to acknowledge the problem. For those wishing to explore patterns of language change through an examination of census returns there is a further difficulty. In previous censuses the question asked was not 'can' but 'does' the person speak, read or write Welsh?. In this latter instance the question could well have been interpreted as being one of customary usage rather than of ability. Clearly the possibility of a lack of concordance between earlier censuses and that of 2001 cannot be dismissed. Again, there is nothing that can be done about this change, although it is very unlikely that the earlier question was ever interpreted in reality as one of usage, and certainly not in modern times.

It is perhaps a paradox that a book on the Welsh language is written in English, especially when, rather like rugby referees at a static maul, language activists demand 'use it or lose it'. Oddly enough, the earliest geographical analysis of the language was actually written in French and published in a French journal (Lewis, 1926). The authors have published in Welsh elsewhere, but the set of studies cited above have all been written in English. To a degree, of course, this stance repeats that of earlier days when even university Departments of Welsh lectured on the language in English. Even that great protagonist of the language, Alwyn Rees, published his seminal work on Welsh rural sociology, *Life in a Welsh Countryside*, in English. This probably marks out one of the old domains where scholarly work was published in an international language. But we make no apology in attempting to make these findings as widely available as possible, for they are vital to all the people of Wales, Welsh-speaking or not.

This book attempts to offer a dispassionate analysis of a so-called minority (or lesser-used) language, but it is clear that no work in this sphere can be value-free. Our standpoint is one of complete support for the language and for its future well-being. Furthermore, we hope that the matters discussed will contribute to on-going debates and be of some interest to policy makers. That said, we are not primarily concerned here with issues of policy. Thus, there is no lengthy discourse on such contentious matters as the means of increasing access to affordable housing in rural areas or controlling in-migration. We do, however, make a brief critical comment on the Welsh Assembly Government's document *Our Language : Its Future* since its recommendations are inevitably related to the conclusions we draw from our analyses.

The Welsh Assembly Government has recently sponsored an organisation 'Culturenet Cymru' to provide access on the internet to an assemblage of material from the museums and galleries of Wales. It has been given the title 'Gathering the Jewels'. We believe that the crown into which all these jewels fit is the Welsh language.

John Aitchison and Harold Carter
Aberystwyth
2004

Acknowledgement

The census data and associated GIS 'shape' files used in this study were made available through the Office for National Statistics. This Crown copyright material is reproduced with the permission of the Controller of HMSO (National Statistics website: www.statistics.gov.uk).

The authors are grateful to Dr Roy Lewis, former Head of the Department of Geography, University of Wales, Aberystwyth for casting a critical eye over the final draft of this text.

Place Names

Throughout this text there is a variable usage of English and Welsh versions of place names. There is no standard rule of thumb, but where Welsh spellings have come to be commonly or more formally recognized, they have been adopted. Likewise, for ease of description, in referring to particular localities or regions use is occasionally made of the names of former administrative districts or counties.

1. INTRODUCTION

The survival of the Welsh language, both as a mother tongue and as a medium of communication still widely deployed in daily life, is a truly remarkable cultural achievement. Wales was the earliest of the peripheral parts of the United Kingdom to be integrated into the developing English state, effectively in 1284, legally in 1536–42, and it was assumed by many (both within and outside Wales) that the natural course of events would see Welsh eventually succumbing to the dominant language of the realm – English. Writing in 1852 Matthew Arnold averred, 'It must always be the desire of a Government to render its dominions, as far as possible, homogeneous ... sooner or later, the language difference between Wales and England will probably be effaced... an event which is socially and politically desirable' (Jones and Thomas, 1973, 127). That Welsh has survived for so long has been, and often still is, a matter of considerable perplexity to English commentators, rather as if it goes against the proper order of things. The often-quoted entry in the early editions of the Encyclopaedia Britannica, 'For Wales see England' encapsulated an attitude which remains widely prevalent. The resilience of the language, in the face of immense odds, has been largely ignored by non-Welsh social historians, or at best has been accorded only cursory allusion. There are now a growing number of publications explicitly concerned with the British islands (Kearney, 1989; Davies, 1999; Robbins, 2002), but it is still apparently possible to present a history of Britain without a single reference to the endurance of Welsh, and its very distinctive contribution to national identity. Such sins of omission (if not commission) need to be countered, and the language given the profile that it rightly deserves on a broader stage. This is all the more vital at the present time for the language would

10

appear to be poised at a particularly crucial turning point in its history. To take but one indicator of linguistic vitality, the remorseless decline in numbers of Welsh-speakers that characterized the whole of the 20th century would seem to have been stayed. Indeed, from the results of the 2001 census it is possible to talk of a genuine turnaround in the fortunes of the language. For the first time, numbers of speakers are seen to be increasing. Admittedly, the situation is not as clear-cut as it may seem, and some weaknesses are still to be discerned, but there can be no doubt that over recent years very significant advances have been made, and that the ground is being prepared for what should be a sustained revitalization of the language during the new millennium.

In this study the intention is to update previous historical and geographical analyses of the Welsh language (Aitchison and Carter, 2000; Jenkins and Williams, 2000) through a detailed evaluation of the 2001 census returns. Using various language indicators, regional patterns and profiles will be explored, and consideration given to the main forces that have shaped them. The implications of the findings, both for the future of the language and for language planning and policy formulation, will also be briefly addressed. Before entering into the main body of the analysis, however, it is appropriate by way of introduction, and for the general reader, to trace some of the major developments that have characterized the evolution of the language, particularly over the past fifty years.

Language Change in Wales : An Overview

To a large extent the recent history of the Welsh language has been determined by the dramatic changes that have taken place in Welsh society and in the restructuring of the Welsh economy. After the Second World War serious losses were recorded in both the number and proportion of Welsh-speakers, with a nadir being reached in the decade 1961–1971. The proportion of the total population speaking Welsh fell by 5.2 per cent (from 26.0% to 20.8%), while absolute numbers of speakers collapsed

11

by a massive 17.3 per cent. The situation seemed dire. As it turned out, however, the decade that followed saw a tempering of the pace of decline. During the period 1981–91 the percentage of Welsh-speakers fell by only 0.3 per cent (from 18.9% to 18.6%), and actual numbers by just 1.4 per cent.

This was the picture at national level; the situation varied considerably across the country. Thus, the greatest falls in percentages and numbers occurred in those areas surrounding, and on the edge of, the core Welsh-speaking areas of the rural north and west (henceforth also referred to as the 'heartland', 'Y Fro Gymraeg' or Welsh-Wales). In the core itself a complex pattern of decreases and increases applied, but it was evident that in many areas the language was in retreat, largely as a result of the steady in-migration of non-Welsh-speakers. The once continuous expanse of the language 'heartland' started to fracture and fragment at key points (Aitchison and Carter, 2000). At the same time, and in sharp, incongruous contrast, the highly Anglicized and urban areas of the country were returning increases in numbers of Welsh-speakers. The increases in the former 'marcher territories' were not yet sufficient to compensate for the losses recorded elsewhere, but they did bode well for the future.

The above outline of the changing geography of the language states the situation very starkly, but it does raise crucial questions and presents a basic paradox. The questions relate to the causes which lie behind the evidence of at least a partial transformation in the well-being of the language – from a state in which imminent demise was forecast to one where regeneration is nascent, albeit within the context of a new spatial order. Further confirmation of the strength of these developments came from a report by Euromosaic in which Welsh was recorded as scoring fairly well on a scale measure of minority languages, and was noted as affording 'some optimism concerning language use' (Nelde, Strubell and Williams, 1996). The paradox, already highlighted, is that the greatest increases had been achieved in those areas where the language had traditionally been weakest. Some explanation of these changes is clearly needed. To a degree this has to be carried out by examining what Nelde, Strubell and Williams argue is the continually changing basis of language groups. 'Our starting point is to develop a conceptualisation of the changing nature of language groups. Thus, rather than resorting to the static concepts of language maintenance and language shift, with their reification of language, we resort to a conception based on the reproduction, production and non-production of language groups. This has the advantage of relating these three processes to the more general processes of social and cultural reproduction' (Nelde, Strubell and Williams, 1996, 5). Arising from these principles it is necessary to consider the way in which those processes of social and cultural reproduction, and consequent language reproduction, have been conditioned by fundamental economic changes on which they, in turn, are based.

G.E. and K. Lang gave their book, which examined '*The President, the Press and the Polls during Watergate*', the title '*The Battle for Public Opinion*' (Lang, G.E. and K, 1983). It would not be inapt to summarise the process of language revival in Wales under the same heading – the battle for public opinion – for it is the control of that public opinion which has impacted most upon the processes of reproduction. But, again, that struggle over opinion has to be set within a very distinctive political and socio-economic context which has been critical to its nurturing.

The political background can be succinctly described as post-modern. Traditionally, in the past neither of the major political parties in Britain had a great regard for the Welsh language. To Conservatives it was no more than a rural patois; to get on, to ascend the greasy pole, to obtain wealth and social influence, English was essential. Welsh was at best an irrelevance, at worst an actual hindrance. What Matthew Arnold had written in the second half of the nineteenth century was still believed at the end of the twentieth century. 'The Welsh language is the curse of Wales. Its prevalence, and the ignorance of the English language, have excluded, and even now exclude the Welsh people from the civilisation of their English neighbours'; and again, 'the sooner the Welsh language disappears as an instrument of the practical, political, social life of Wales, the better…' (Arnold, 1867). On the other hand, socialism's main concern was with internationalism, with brother workers and comrades in Britain and elsewhere. As Ieuan Gwynedd Jones has written, 'From 1911 onwards socialism and the new miners' union were becoming the new religion. The language of socialism was English… To abandon Welsh became not only a valuational but also a symbolic gesture of rejection and affirmation – rejection of the political philosophy and the sham combination of Lib-Labism and the affirmation of new solidarities and new idealisms based upon a secular and anti-religious philosophy. Fifty years earlier the new unions of the coalfield had issued their pamphlets, transacted their business, and organized themselves politically in Welsh. *The Miners' Next Step* was written in English and never translated into Welsh' (Jones, 1992, 178). The medium of communication became English, and Welsh, therefore, with its associations with Liberalism and nonconformity, a marginal relic of little matter. Indeed, the attitude of some supporters of Labour was not very different from that of Arnold. It was against that socio-cultural background, and the location of socio-economic power in the hands of those who saw little relevance in it, that the decline of the language which marked much of the last century took place.

But the end of the twentieth century witnessed an ideological sea-change. The dogmatic certainties of both right and left were relinquished as the one brought increasing social division and created a disaffected underclass, and the other, as evident in eastern Europe, brought economic atrophy and social decay. In consequence there has been the substitution of a pragmatism in which the clash of ideologies, within which attitudes to the language were emplaced, has been minimised, so that conflicts of principle become centred on specific, single issues rather than on grand designs. That said, it still appears in the Labour Party where the nostalgia for socialism continues to demonstrate a reaction against the pragmatism of Government. But it was into such a situation that the so-called single issue fanatics were able to insert their concerns. Animal rights, pro-life anti-abortion, gun control, environmental matters such as anti-road building or anti-GM crops, all these have dominated the news. And one of these issues was (and continues to be) that of the Welsh language, as propagated mainly by *Cymdeithas Yr Iaith Gymraeg* (The Welsh Language Society). The Society, indeed, was one of the earliest of the protagonists of a single issue, for it was founded in its present form in 1962 following a BBC lecture by Saunders Lewis entitled '*Tynged yr Iaith*' or '*The Fate of the Language*' (Lewis, 1962; Jones and Thomas, 1973). But it became legitimised as one amongst a number of quite disparate groups, for language activists could be matched with those who forcibly propounded other matters. Moreover, the peak of direct action was in the late 1960s when parallel anti-establishment movements were on the move across western Europe. In essence, language activists appeared now as one of many comparable groups, part of a general stir rather than a set of isolated oddities as they had often been regarded in the past.

At the same time Wales was undergoing a major economic transformation. It can be epitomised by the single term, de-industrialization. The old heavy industries, especially coal and iron and steel, were in the process of decline or rationalisation. Employment patterns were radically changing, and in place of the decaying smoke-stack industries new fields of work were expanding. These were in the services, bureaucracy and the media. In a survey of the Welsh economy Blackaby *et alia* observed, 'as for the total distribution of employment in Wales, the largest employing sector is the service sector, where roughly seven out of every ten employees are employed... the overall picture... is one of a service-sector based economy... the traditional heavy industry playing a small role in industrial employment' (Blakaby *et alia*, 1995, 236). Between 1992 and 1995 employment in agriculture in Wales fell by 5 per cent; in energy- and water-based industries it collapsed by 27 per cent. In contrast, employment in banking and finance rose by nearly 20 per cent. Whereas in the past the conflict between owner/manager and worker had neatly-fitted the parties of the right and the left, now a new bourgeoisie which was partly Welsh-speaking was being created. It was made up of the people who operated the social and health services, who ran the enlarged and increasingly complex system of government in Wales which followed the creation of the Welsh Office in 1964 and the Welsh Assembly after the referendum of 1997, and who contributed in a major way to the development of education from *Ysgol Feithrin* (nursery school) to University. The same changes were responsible, too, for the greatly enhanced status and scale of the mass media. Into the jobs thus created moved Welshmen and women, mainly educated in Wales and many of them able to speak the language. They formed a new Welsh-speaking sector, high on the social scale and with very different attitudes to the language from those which had been dominant at the beginning of the century.

The radical re-structuring of agriculture had a particularly dramatic impact on rural communities. The capitalization of farming systems and the substitution of machinery for labour prompted a drift from the land and contributed to the on-going process of rural depopulation; a process that has been endemic since the last quarter of the nineteenth century. Small farms became uneconomic and amalgamations resulted. In 1971 there were 16,810 holdings under 20 hectares, by 1996 the number had fallen to 10,977. During the same period numbers of regular whole-time hired workers on farms fell from 6,529 to 2,721 (Welsh Office, 1997, 174/5). Between 2000 and 2001 employment in the primary sector as a whole fell by almost 19 per cent (Brooksbank, 2002). In January 2001 *The Western Mail* reported that in Wales farming jobs (full-time and part-time) were being lost at the rate of 73 per week, and that 3,800 fewer were employed in June 2000 than at the same time in the previous year (January 16, 2001, *Country and Farming*, 1). With the displacement of

16

these workers out-migration gathered pace. Moreover, that out-migration was largely age-specific, removing the young and the active and, among them, Welsh-speakers. Like the sons and daughters of miners and steel workers, the children of farmers looked, often via higher education, for employment in the growing service occupations and moved to where they were concentrated. In addition, the diminution of numbers in the countryside had a damaging impact upon services with chapels, schools, post offices, village shops and pubs all being lost. In brief, the old tightly-knit rural communities within which the Welsh language was an integral element were shattered. But from the language point of view worse was to follow. By the 1970s the process known as counter-urbanisation was under way. Many people living in the metropolises and large towns had become disillusioned with the environment of congestion, pollution and crime, and with a way of life dominated by materialism and competition. They sought change by moving to what was imagined to be the more congenial physical and social environment of rural areas, and rural Wales became a target area for such movements. There followed a re-population which in numerical terms offset the underlying depopulation and in many places yielded net gains. But these were of a new population, to a degree an alien one. Inevitably, such demographic movements impacted on the relative strength of the language, and most especially in the core Welsh-speaking areas. So much so, that there is now no way in which the old Welsh-speaking communities can be recreated, for the whole economic system and its social bases have been profoundly transformed and reconstituted.

All of these trends, political and economic, which severely buffeted Welsh society, were certainly not divorced one from the other. The young language activists of the sixties have become more mature operators of the system and parents of the Welsh-speaking children demanding Welsh-medium education. The changing nature of the economy provided an opportunity for those committed to the language for lodgement in positions of influence. The crucial aspect of those positions of influence was the way in which the battle for public opinion could be manipulated. The field of that battle was, and continues to be, the mass media.

At this point in the discussion, and with the political and socio-economic background which has been broadly outlined in mind, it is appropriate to turn to a consideration of some of the key themes enunciated by the Langs concerning the battle for public opinion (Lang, G.E. and K, 1983), and to relate these to language issues in Wales. The first of these themes is the setting of the agenda. 'The agenda-setting hypothesis derives from the observation that the mass media, whilst perhaps not very effective in persuading people <u>what</u> to think, do seem to tell people what to think about' (Lang and Lang, 1983, 7). McCombs and Shaw describe the agenda-setting function in the same manner – that people learn from the mass media what the important issues are (McCombs and Shaw, 1972). As far as the Welsh language is concerned, a formal way of measuring that function would be to determine the time devoted to language issues by news and current affairs programmes of BBC Wales, Radio Cymru and HTV or in the columns of *The Western Mail*. Such an analysis, with necessary recourse to transcripts of broadcasts over a long period – a form of content analysis – is hardly feasible. But there is little doubt that, anecdotally at least, it is possible to maintain that the language was made into an issue put continually before the public. That the media are fully convinced that they control the agenda can be discerned in an advertisement in *The Western Mail* on Thursday, February 12, 1997, for an editor for the programme 'Wales Today', described as the 'BBC Wales flagship news programme'. The job description states bluntly, 'it sets the news agenda for Wales'. The newspapers followed along with radio and television, and the language became a standby topic for discussion. The Welsh-speaking bourgeoisie, whose rise has already been traced, played a significant role in the decision-making echelons of the media and was consistently able to insert the language into the agenda of matters of public importance, and furthermore to keep it there.

18

Alongside setting the agenda, there is another theoretical notion, referred to as the 'refraction principle'. This suggests that against the background of the increasing mass of news and information which is generated, most people have neither the time nor the expertise to develop informed views; they are reliant on the media. But not only do the media select which matters to bring forward, those matters are inevitably presented in a specific way. Most social scientists would accept the idea that, however honest the intention, there is no such thing as objectivity. That is, the information stream is refracted through the mediation of editors and presenters. And, in the case of the language, those who were setting the agenda were also to some degree the presenters. Public opinion was, therefore, steered away from the attitude which had dominated the language over the last century or more, where Welsh was perceived as a dying language best left to decay, to one of committed support, or at the very least of tacit acceptance.

A third theoretical determinant of public opinion is the significance of so-called 'critical events' (Lang and Lang, 1983, 9). This argument maintains that opinion can be tangibly directed by specific events which become 'causes célèbres' and sway judgements. In relation to the language two can be selected by way of illustration. Perhaps the most significant was the drowning of Capel Celyn and the Tryweryn valley, and the creation of Llyn Celyn in 1963 for water supply, by the city of Liverpool. Of the Welsh members of Parliament 27 out of 36 voted against the Bill when it was introduced in 1957; none voted for it. But it was carried against what can be fairly described as the unanimous opposition of Welsh people. Trevor Fishlock, an English journalist, wrote, 'the episode of Tryweryn was a traumatic one and is one of the keys to what has been happening in Wales in recent years. From it sprang a great anger and a hardening of resolve; for many men and women it was an awakening, the first indication that the values of Wales were in danger and were meaningless to the authorities in England' (Fishlock, 1972, 102). Or as one member of

Cymdeithas Yr Iaith put it, '*Daeth brwydr Tryweryn yn sumbol o'r frwydr dros hawliau iaith, hawliau cymdeithas a hawliau cenedl*' (Tudur, 1989, 16). ('The struggle for Tryweryn became a symbol of the struggle for the rights of the language, the rights of community and the rights of the nation.') The demonstrable arrogance and the crude manifestation of the English dominance of Wales built up a resentment which was released not in direct political terms, for Plaid Cymru has had only limited electoral success, but in renewed feelings of warmth towards the language. Perhaps this was because the language was an easily identifiable single issue as opposed to the complexities of political convictions, especially where, as has already been argued, in post-modern Wales formal political conflict seemed related to degree of administrative competence rather than ideology. But, in addition, the language can be seen as the only obvious remaining symbol of Welsh difference and identity. Even for the non-Welsh-speakers the language could be a symbol. And if they did not speak it, their children could. The dramatic increases in the numbers of young Welsh-speakers between 1981 and 1991 was clear evidence of a growing reaction. Six of the eight counties, as they then were, recorded increases of over 30 per cent in the age group 3–15 years; indeed, three counties recorded increases of double that figure.

Along with Tryweryn another attitude-shaping event was the creation in 1982 of the fourth Welsh language television channel, S4C as it became known. The channel had been promised by the Conservative Party in its manifesto, but on coming into power it prepared to renege on the commitment. The subsequent threat of the President of Plaid Cymru to fast to death, and the pressure from a group of prominent Welshmen, reversed the decision. The outcome was the opposite of that for Tryweryn, a victory for Wales over the English establishment, and the direct issue of that victory was the language.

It is interesting to observe that two other earlier 'critical events' seemed to have had only a limited impact upon general public opinion. The attempt to inflict what was little more than symbolic damage on a Bombing School at Penyberth near Pwllheli by three Welsh nationalists in 1936, and the subsequent switching of the trial from Caernarfon to London after the jury failed to reach a verdict, has been called by Dafydd Jenkins, 'Something of a turning point in the revival of Welsh national consciousness' (Jenkins, 1998, xiii). Yet even Jenkins uses the qualification 'something of', and the impact on attitudes to the language across Wales at large seems to have been very limited, some indeed were hostile. Likewise the requisitioning by the army of a large area of Mynydd Epynt in 1940, with the eviction of some 219 adults and children, caused but little concern (Hughes, 1998). It is true that both these events occurred under the threat from Nazi Germany which certainly influenced attitudes. But what the limited reaction to these threats to the integrity of language in rural Wales epitomises is the crucial nature of the changed economic and social environment in the second half of the last century. To have impact that changed condition was essential.

The clearest indication of the success in the later battle for public opinion, and in the winning over of non-Welsh-speakers, comes in the poll conducted for the Welsh Language Board in 1996 (Welsh Language Board, 1996). It reported that 84 per cent of the sample who were Welsh-speaking supported the Board's aim, 'to enable the language to become self-sustaining and secure as a medium of communication in Wales', and that 96 per cent of the Welsh-speakers and 94 per cent of the non-Welsh-speakers agreed with the view that numbers of Welsh-speakers should be increased. Again, 94 per cent of the Welsh-speakers and 80 per cent of the non-Welsh-speakers were of the opinion that more opportunities to use the language should be provided (Welsh Language Board, 1996, 2–3). All of these data underline how attitudes appear to have been won over, and a firm basis for growth provided.

The discussion thus far has been largely concerned with the fight to control public opinion. It was vital that the success achieved on this front was turned into real gains in the field of education. The history of the development of Welsh-medium education is far too large an issue to be dealt with effectively here; it is however of fundamental significance. Suffice it to note that the first Welsh-medium primary school was established at Aberystwyth in 1939, although it was independent and did not come under the Local Education Authority until 1951. The first Local Education Authority Welsh-medium primary school was opened at Llanelli in 1947. In the decades that followed teaching through the medium of Welsh at primary school level increased steadily, with the pace quickening from the 1970s onwards. Of the 1624 primary schools in Wales in 2001/2, 442 (27 per cent) were mainly Welsh-medium schools, with a further 80 (5 per cent) teaching parts of the curriculum through Welsh. In the remaining 1,102 schools (68 per cent) Welsh was taught as a second language. The proportion of all pupils (281,275) in each of these three categories of primary school were 18.2, 2.4 and 79.4, respectively. While it was estimated that nearly 17 per cent of primary school pupils were fluent in Welsh (c.f. 13 per cent in 1988), significantly of these only 37 per cent spoke Welsh at home. Between 1988 and 2001 the proportion of pupils who were taught Welsh as a first language also increased, in this case from 9 per cent to nearly 15 per cent. The first Welsh-medium secondary school (Ysgol Glan Clwyd) was established at Rhyl by Flintshire County Council in 1956. At the present time there are 53 secondary schools in Wales where six subjects or more are taught through the Welsh language; in 1990/1 there were 44. Of the 229 secondary schools maintained by LEAs in 2001/2, 72 taught Welsh as a first and a second language. In the remainder Welsh was taught only as a second language. In 1987 just 42 per cent of secondary school children (years 7–11) were taught Welsh as a second language; by 2002 this had increased to nearly 85 per cent. These developments have clearly impacted on the strength of the language nationally, for Welsh is now a compulsory subject for all pupils in Wales. This means that all pupils study Welsh (either as a first or a second language) for 11 years, from the ages of 5 to 16. A further initiative of note in the educational sphere has been the formation of a network of Welsh-medium nursery schools (Stevens, 1996). This movement began in 1949 at Maesteg. It grew slowly at first, but by 1970 had led to the establishment of some 60 Ysgolion Meithrin (Nursery Schools) in all parts of Wales. Such was the success of the initiative that by 1995 the number of nursery schools had reached 625, with a further 379 'mother and child' groups. Pertinently, a high proportion of the children attending these schools are from non-Welsh-speaking homes. The University of Wales and other institutes of higher education in Wales have responded to the success of the Welsh-medium schools. Since the late 1960s courses and degrees through the medium of Welsh have been offered at Aberystwyth and Bangor, as have teacher-training programmes. The domain of education, which had been lost during the nineteenth century, has been effectively reclaimed, even if not yet to the satisfaction of many language activists. The promotion of Welsh as either a first and or a second language throughout the school system was a major achievement. So much so, that in certain fields it is now possible to move from nursery education to post-doctoral research largely within the Welsh language.

Equally in the public domain, the official reinstatement of the language has reversed the restrictions first imposed at the Act of Union in 1536. That, too, has been a long and complex process, culminating in the Welsh Language Act of 1993. This not only ensured equality of Welsh with English before the law, but set up a permanent Welsh Language Board 'to promote and facilitate the use of the Welsh language'. The Act states that every public body which provides services to the public in Wales or exercises statutory functions in relation to the provision by other public bodies of services to the public in Wales, shall prepare a scheme specifying the measures it proposes to take as to the use of Welsh, 'so far as it is both appropriate in the circumstances and reasonably practical'. It ensures the right to use Welsh in the law courts, as long as due notice is given, and dictates that all official forms and circulars are issued in Welsh. All this is overseen by the Language Board which in 1996 published '*A Strategy for the Welsh Language*'. This strategy identifies the means by which the Board would seek to implement its remit to promote and facilitate the use of the Welsh language and 'to enable the Welsh language to be self-sustaining and secure as a medium of communication in Wales'. Twenty objectives were put forward and the Board's role and responsibility in each outlined, together with a comment on the task of realising them and a listing of partners in the process. The very existence of the strategy is further evidence of the degree to which attitudes to the language have been effectively transformed over the last quarter of a century.

But if the language has become more and more accepted as the basis of Welsh identity, and has support from speakers and non-speakers alike, the traditional means of reproduction have been greatly weakened. The two domains in which Welsh remained most secure during the nineteenth century and the first half of the twentieth were the chapel and the home or the hearth (*yr aelwyd*). However, the late twentieth century has seen an accelerating decline in the influence of nonconformist Christianity and the impact upon Welsh people of the secularism and consumerism of the western way of life. Above all, the Sunday school, which virtually saved the language through the use of the Welsh Bible no longer functions as the provider of an education through the medium of Welsh. In addition, the instability of marriage, as well as the greater frequency of linguistically 'mixed marriages' which is partly a function of greater mobility, have undermined the effectiveness of the home. Moreover, distance and inaccessibility, which once constituted the great defences of the language in the community, no longer have any meaning in an electronic age. Radio, television and the internet have brought English, even if it is American English, onto the hearth.

The relationship between household structures and the long-term well-being of the language has been analysed in statistical detail by Aitchison and Carter (2000, 127–132) for the 1991 census, and the complex findings need not be repeated here. It is sufficient to note that at the time while 26 per cent of households in Wales contained at least one Welsh-speaker, of these only 54 per cent were wholly Welsh-speaking. Significantly, this 54 per cent was comprised mainly of households without children. Only 11 per cent of households with Welsh-speakers were wholly Welsh-speaking and had children. These, and other data, prompted the conclusion that 'For the moment … the domain of the family and the home cannot be regarded as a major stimulus for the maintenance and reproduction of the language. Welsh-speaking households are fractured and structurally diverse in composition' (Aitchison and Carter, 2000, 132).

The implication which follows from the decline of the chapel and the limitation of the family as the key progenitors of the language is that other sources of support have had to be relied upon. These are the ones which have already received comment. The Welsh language schools, as well as facilities for adult learning, have become the real basis of a Welsh language renaissance. Their impact has been boosted further by the Welsh language media. In brief, in contemporary Wales new or renewed bases for language reproduction have replaced the traditional and declining bases.

It would be wrong, however, to give the impression that resistance to this language revival does not exist. The survey for the Welsh Language Board, already quoted, certainly suggests a general backing, but there are strident voices still raised if not in direct opposition at least in a questioning mode. They are well represented in a quotation from Giggs and Pattie. 'There seems to be evidence of a cultural elitism among some Welsh-speaking Welsh people. It is heartening that proficiency in Britain's oldest language (hitherto long derided) now provides dignity, social prestige and opportunity in Wales. At the same time it is profoundly disheartening that a few zealots can seriously assert that the English-speaking majority, who constitute 77.6 per cent of the Welsh-born residents in 1981… are 'not *really* Welsh'. Moreover, the problems are not simply those of proficiency in the Welsh language being touted as the essential qualification Welsh nationality, rather than mere nativity, which is deemed a sufficient qualification in the majority of countries: there are attendant cultural, political and economic implications'. (Giggs and Pattie, 1991, 29). These views can be taken to more extreme lengths. A case in point is a characteristic attack by Professor Christie Davies of the Social Affairs Unit as reported in *The Western Mail* for January 28, 1997. In this the author of an article called 'Loyalty Misplaced' is said to call for 'euthanasia of an already-dying language and immediate removal of bilingual signs' (Betts, 1997, 1). This re-echoes the view of Matthew Arnold quoted earlier and noted as being still extant. The argument of those who agree with Giggs and Pattie, but who might not go quite as far as Davies, is that out of the whole set of arrangements for the governance of Wales, including the existing national institutions such as the University, the Library and the Museum, and of course the Welsh Office and now including the Welsh Assembly, a distinctive Welsh set of institutions will emerge from which the identity of Wales will be eventually derived, an identity which will be independent of language. This has a close link with Gwyn Williams's question of '*When Was Wales?*'. 'Wales is an artefact which the Welsh produce; the Welsh make and remake Wales day by day and year after year' (Williams,G.A, 1979). Such a Wales will be more akin to Ireland where, although conventional obeisance is made to the Irish language, that language plays little real part in the national identity of the country. Such identity is derived from political freedom and independence, and from the development of specific Irish institutions. In such a way a Welsh identity, based on distinctive institutions, will be more securely formed, and will include all the people who wish to call themselves Welsh and not only the limited number who are Welsh-speaking. Interestingly, and in contrast to this view, Roberts reports from a study in Blaina and Nant-y-glo, 'in summary, there seems to be an emergent, stronger sense of cultural nationalism rather than a discernible trend towards national self-determination as a political demand' (Roberts, 1994, 89).

It is apparent that the conflict over language that characterised Wales in the past is not resolved. It spills over, of course, into the perennial conflict over whether Welshness depends on geographic location, personal sentiment, or cultural identity as determined by language. It is because of the last of these – equating Welshness with the language – that the emerging revival which has been traced here is still regarded with suspicion, if not with downright opposition. But the advantage, as far as public opinion (or, in other terms, social and cultural reproduction) is concerned, no longer rests exclusively with those who would seek to eliminate Welsh. It is on this that its revival has depended. Moreover, it is now primarily an urban and secular language better equipped to cope with the demands of the new century. But if, as Nelde, Strubell and Williams maintain, 'the concepts of language production and reproduction relate to three primary agencies – the family, education and community' (Nelde, Strubell and Williams 1996, 6), with the media being a further agency, then it would appear that in the case of Welsh the family has become a much less certain agency than once it was, whilst the conflict within the community, arbitrated by the media, will determine the course of education, a prime basis of contemporary reproduction.

It is to be appreciated that what has been outlined and interpreted here, is no more, and no less, than a stage in the process of the language's history. The crucial issue behind what success has been achieved, behind the foundation of the impressive infrastructure of support highlighted above, as indeed it was behind the long decline, has been access to power within the country and through it the ability to influence public opinion and attitudes. At the very heart of much of the discussion of the language has been the notion of culture, and Welsh culture is often interpreted as an artefact in its own right. But it can be argued that culture itself is not a discrete and independent thing, 'an ontological given' (Mitchell, 1995), but rather a complex created in order to advance power bases. Mitchell contends that social theorists must 'dispense with the notion of an ontological culture and begin focusing instead on how the very idea of culture has been developed and deployed as a means of attempting to order, control and define "others" in the name of power and profit' (Mitchell. 1995, 104). Again he maintains that 'culture... comes to signify artificial distinctiveness where in reality there is always contest and flux. What gets called "culture" is created through struggles by groups and individuals possessing radically different access to power' (Mitchell, 1995, 108). If this be so then the fight for the language has not been won for, of necessity, there is a continuing tension between the conflicting interests of population groups in Wales in relation to the language. Crudely this appears in the pro- and anti-language letters which appear with regularity in the correspondence columns of *The Western Mail*. But those are but the superficial manifestations of the underlying conflict and of the struggle for control of the levers of power. Such esoteric matters are of relevance to the present study, for the findings of the 2001 census that are to be examined here, should not be seen as simply an isolated data set, but more as an indicator of the direction which the struggle to maintain the language is taking; for however critical the bases of the 'reproduction, production and non-production of language groups' may be, a careful monitoring and evaluation of the contemporary state of the language and its geographical expression is also essential. This is particularly the case at the present time since the changes that had been forecast to take place during the last decade of the 20th century were thought to presage a major step-change in the fortunes in language.

Writing in the late 1980s, and basing their conclusions on the evidence of the censuses from 1961 to 1981, the present authors suggested that 'numbers of Welsh-speakers will continue to decline until the year 2001, but thereafter there will be a notable reversal of the trend, with numbers increasing sharply'. They went on to suggest, however, that 'Whilst this scenario augers well for the language, it is based on a major reshaping of the geography of language distribution… The predicted overall turnaround in numbers of Welsh-speakers by the year 2001 is explained by a continuance of the rapid advances recently recorded in the borderland areas of Wales, and in particular the increases that could be returned in main urban centres'. The growth experienced in these areas, it was argued, could 'more than compensate for the small absolute losses that are likely to happen in the most vulnerable parts of rural Wales, as well as the more serious decline that could take place in those industrial regions of West Glamorgan and south-east Dyfed' (Aitchison and Carter, 1991). If these predictions were to be fulfilled, then the 2001 census would mark a truly defining moment in the history of the Welsh language. Decline might well continue to apply (albeit at a reduced rate) within the traditional heartland of the north and west (Welsh-Wales), but at national level these would be out-weighed by the increases expected elsewhere (Anglo-Wales). As a result, and for the first time in over a century, one could contemplate a veritable renaissance of the language – at least as portrayed in census enumerations. This was certainly not a situation envisaged by Saunders Lewis in his hard-hitting 1962 radio-broadcast – '*Tynged yr Iaith*' (The Fate of the Language). With great foreboding, he was moved to state:

'*Mi ragdybiaf hefyd y bydd terfyn ar y Gymraeg yn iaith fyw… tua dechrau'r unfed ganrif ar hugain.*' ('*I shall also presuppose that Welsh will end as a living language… about the beginning of the twenty-first century.*') (Lewis, 1962, 5)

But this was his prediction, '*should the present trend continue*' ('*ond parhau'r tueddiad presennol*'). As it happened, and in no small measure due to his forthright 'call to action', during the 1980s and 1990s there was a notable deceleration in the pace of decline, to the point where it was possible to look forward to a more broadly-based advance rather than a terminal retreat. Whether or not such trends inevitably imply a strengthening of Welsh as 'a living language' is, however, a different and debatable matter.

The main intention of the statistical analysis that follows is to determine the degree to which these forecasts made for the language at the turn of the millennium have been realised, and in so doing to consider the implications of the findings for the future of the language in general, and for policy formulation in particular. This is effected through a largely map-based investigation of the various tabulations published by the Office of National Statistics from the 2001 census.

2. THE 2001 CENSUS

As is always the case with censuses of population, caveats and qualifications have to be made regarding the nature and treatment of the data generated. This applies most particularly in considering trends over time and associated changes in regional patterns. Such technical matters are addressed within the body of the discussion as it unfolds below. It is worth noting at the outset, however, that reference will be made to a variety of published census tabulations. These include 'Census Area Statistics' (CAS), standard tables and theme tables. Frustratingly, because of the way in which they have been derived and because of internal controls on the disclosure of confidential information, these tabulations and cross-tabulations can yield slightly differing figures for seemingly the same variables (e.g. numbers of Welsh-speakers). Such differences are, however, often not of major consequence and can be accommodated in a broad overview study such as this. The various tabulations also refer to differing 'geographical' areas, mainly because of differences in so-called threshold limits. These limits specify the minimum number of people and households that need to be enumerated in an area before particular sets of data can be disclosed. Thus, in the compilation of standard tables for electoral divisions in Wales (the equivalent of 'wards' in England), the areas concerned must have at least 400 households and a resident population of at least 1000. An electoral division that fails to meet these criteria has to be amalgamated with a neighbouring electoral division within the same local authority. The CAS threshold for an electoral division is less demanding – 100 people and 40 households. In Wales the CAS tabulations are for 881 electoral divisions, while for standard tables they are for 868 (13 electoral divisions being amalgamated). Both these spatial frames are used in this study. It has been noted that the Office for National Statistics uses the term 'electoral division' in Wales, while in England the equivalent administrative area is referred to as a 'ward'. Since the latter term has been widely-used in past studies of Welsh census data, and is still commonly deployed, the decision has been taken to use it, rather the more clumsy descriptor – electoral division – in the presentation that follows.

As in previous censuses in Wales, those enumerated at the 2001 census were requested to indicate whether or not they could speak, read or write Welsh. A notable addition, however, was the inclusion for the first time of a new item concerning the ability to 'understand' Welsh. The structure of the language question was such that, theoretically, respondents could check any combination of the boxes for these four language skills; in the jargon, it was a multiple response question. To simplify tabulation of the resultant data, the National Statistics Office elected in the CAS listings to derive five key combinations of responses, together with a catch-all, residual category. The six language categories for which data have been published are defined as follows:

(i)   Understands spoken Welsh only
(ii) Speaks, but does not read or write Welsh
(iii) Speaks and reads, but does not write Welsh
(iv) Speaks, reads and writes Welsh
(v)   Other combinations of skills
(vi) No knowledge of Welsh

At the time of writing, the residual category (v) – 'other combinations of skills' – had not been fully disaggregated. This creates some problems, most notably for example in seeking to determine patterns of literacy. All that can be said at this stage is that the 2001 census identified 83,662 persons with some knowledge of the Welsh language, the precise nature of which is not disclosed. However, it is worth mentioning in this regard that for the 1991 census two other categories were defined which identified those who were 'able to read, but not speak or write Welsh' and those who were 'able to read and write, but not speak Welsh'. *Faute de mieux*, it is assumed here that the 'other combinations of skills' category mainly embraces these latter two definitions. However, it would appear from other data published as standard tables that this category also includes some Welsh-speakers (see below).

For each of the six language categories listed above, data for Wales are collated at various spatial scales – national, local authority (22), wards (881) and so-called output areas (9769). Much of the analysis presented here is based on the mapping of data for wards. It has to be emphasized, however, that these vary greatly in size, and that their boundaries have been subject to change over the period 1991–2001. Both of these factors constrain discussion of spatial variations and associated trends (e.g. changes in numbers of Welsh-speakers). The configuration of wards for CAS tabulations is depicted in Figure 1.

Before considering the statistics for the first three of the spatial formats identified above, and for the full set of CAS language variables, it needs to be noted that, as in recent censuses, the language data relate specifically to those who were resident and aged three years and over at the time of the enumeration (April 29th, 2001). For this particular segment of the population the number recorded in Wales was 2,805,701 (c.f. 2,723,623 in 1991). It should be stressed, however, that the figure for 2001 includes all students who were attending centres of higher education in Wales at the time of the census. Significantly, for the 1991 census, such students were enumerated at their home rather than their term-time addresses. This difference in the definition of the respective base populations is clearly of particular relevance when considering local patterns of language change, since these would be greatly affected by the differential movement in and out of Welsh- and non-Welsh-speaking students. Such matters will manifest themselves most obviously in university towns, but they will inevitably

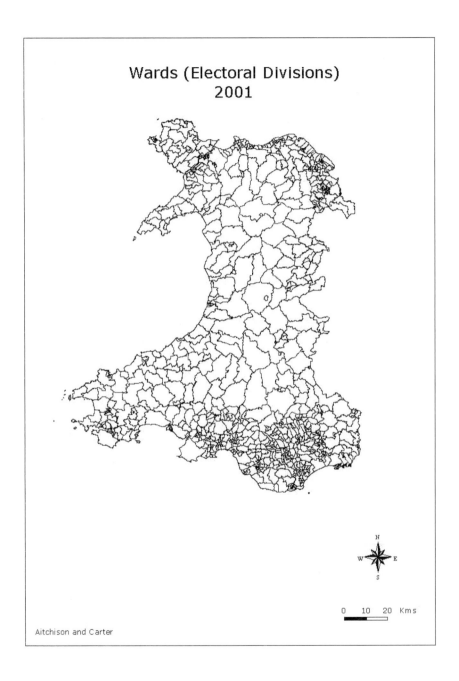

Wards (Electoral Divisions)
2001

Aitchison and Carter

Figure 1.

have an impact on all areas – albeit to varying degrees. With this caveat duly recognized, Table 1 records absolute numbers for each of the language categories for Wales and the 22 local authority areas. These data are also expressed in percentage forms in Table 2 and Table 3.

One further point needs to be added. The census authorities have steadfastly refused to enumerate Welsh-speakers in areas of the United Kingdom outside of Wales. Accordingly, the statistics detailed in this study do not represent the totality of the Welsh-speaking population. All that can be said, is that there were 629,000 persons recorded as born in Wales, but who were living in other parts of the United Kingdom at the time of the 2001 census enumeration. This figure includes Welsh students attending centres of higher education outside of Wales. Needless to say, it would be of considerable interest to know precisely what proportion of this substantial expatriate community would claim an ability to understand, speak, read and/or write Welsh.

3. KNOWLEDGE AND UNDERSTANDING OF THE WELSH LANGUAGE

Taken together, the first five language categories identify those who have a 'knowledge' of the Welsh language (i.e. those who have at least one skill in the language). This ranges from a simple understanding of spoken Welsh only to an ability to speak, read and write Welsh, with various other combinations of skills in-between. The 2001 census reveals that 28.4 per cent of the population aged over 3 years in Wales have some knowledge of the Welsh language – 797,717 persons in total (Tables 1 and 2). On the face of it these are very high figures, and would appear to suggest that, nationally, the language has an even firmer hold than previously imagined. Certainly, the addition of a new indicator relating to the 'understanding' of spoken Welsh adds a further dimension to the assessment of the strength of the language – albeit one that presumes a very basic level of ability. At the local authority level four areas can be distinguished where more than 60 per cent of the population have a knowledge of the language – Gwynedd (76.1 per cent), Ynys Môn (70.4 per cent), Carmarthenshire (63.6 per cent) and Ceredigion (61.2 per cent). Significantly, of the other areas only four have percentages of less than 15, and then only marginally so – Torfaen (14.5 per cent), Newport (13.4 per cent), Blaenau Gwent (13.3 per cent) and Monmouthshire (12.9 per cent).

The proportion of resident populations aged 3 and over with a knowledge of Welsh at ward level varies greatly, from a low of 9.6 (Trellech United, Monmouthshire) to a high of 93.9 (Peblig, Gwynedd). Half of all wards record percentages in excess of 22.2. Table 4 and Figure 2 highlight the strongly bi-modal nature of the overall distribution, with a sharp contrast evident between a core area where more than half of the population has a knowledge of Welsh, and a periphery where percentages of less than 20 per cent are widely recorded. A transitional zone between these main areas, with percentages between 20 and 50, can be discerned, but this is attenuated and rather fragmented in form. The highest percentages – 80 and over – are seen to be recorded by wards within the Llŷn Peninsula, central Ynys Môn, Caernarfon and Bangor and the immediate hinterland (including Llanberis), and central Gwynedd (including Trawsfynydd and Llanuwchllyn). In south Wales a small number of wards around Llannon, Pontyberem and Penygroes in south-eastern Carmarthenshire record equally high percentages. For much of the traditional heartland the proportion of the population claiming some knowledge of Welsh ranges between 65 and 79. Although quite extensive, this latter zone is rather fractured in nature, for in many parts it is surrounded and penetrated by wards where percentages are between 50 per cent and 64 per cent. As far as the long-term strength of the language within the heartland is concerned, it is the situation in these weaker areas that is particularly critical. They represent lines or zones of attrition. Of note are the Conwy valley region in north Wales, coastal parts of Meirionnydd and northern Ceredigion (Aberystwyth and Borth), and small clusters of wards within the Llŷn Pensinsula (e.g. around Abersoch and Llanbedrog) and on Ynys Môn (e.g. the Holyhead region, Moelfre, Benllech and Beaumaris). Wards in much of southern Ceredigion and northern Pembrokeshire record similar values. Beyond the Welsh core, knowledge of the language is of a much lower magnitude, with percentages in many areas falling below 20. Throughout Monmouthshire, and in the neighbouring urban districts of Blaenau Gwent, Torfaen, Caerphilly and Newport the percentage of the population claiming a knowledge of Welsh in many localities is under 15. Equally low values are recorded by wards

Table 1
Census Language Categories
Numbers of Persons Aged 3 and Over : 2001

Local Authority Area	Understands Spoken Welsh only	Speaks Welsh, but does not read or write Welsh	Speaks and reads Welsh, but does not write Welsh	Speaks, reads and writes Welsh	Other comb- inations of skills	Knowledge of Welsh (at least one language skill)
Blaenau Gwent	1483	1291	403	4447	1402	9026
Bridgend	5314	2005	1091	10059	6294	24763
Caerphilly	4617	2814	1095	13916	4786	27228
Cardiff	8630	4114	2077	25753	7424	47998
Carmarthenshire	17494	12085	6507	65210	5144	106440
Ceredigion	5211	3635	1990	32147	1652	44635
Conwy	8335	4280	2064	24698	2797	42174
Denbighshire	6350	3297	1566	18677	2579	32469
Flintshire	6296	3051	1520	15656	4137	30660
Gwynedd	6663	6491	2609	68395	1689	85847
Merthyr Tydfil	2180	928	524	3976	1994	9602
Monmouthshire	1691	1319	490	5619	1471	10590
Neath/Port Talbot	8490	4252	2207	16723	5879	37551
Newport	2478	2336	803	9469	2536	17622
Pembrokeshire	5982	3870	1804	18012	2672	32340
Powys	7433	3912	2048	19556	3898	36847
Rhondda Cynon Taf	9530	3724	1868	21913	10178	47213
Swansea	12953	5348	2955	20278	7048	48582
Torfaen	1701	1697	611	7117	1616	12742
Vale of Glamorgan	3357	1802	794	10138	3362	19453
Wrexham	6579	2924	1456	13515	3927	28401
Ynys Môn	5649	4135	1902	32672	1176	45534
Wales	**138416**	**79310**	**38384**	**457946**	**83661**	**797717**

Table 2

Census Language Categories

As a Percentage of Population Aged 3 and Over : 2001

Local AuthorityArea	Understands Spoken Welsh only	Speaks Welsh, but does not read or write Welsh	Speaks and reads Welsh, but does not write Welsh	Speaks, reads and writes Welsh	Other comb- inations of skills	Knowledge of Welsh (at least one language skill)
Blaenau Gwent	2.2	1.9	0.6	6.6	2.1	13.3
Bridgend	4.3	1.6	0.9	8.1	5.1	19.9
Caerphilly	2.8	1.7	0.7	8.5	2.9	16.7
Cardiff	2.9	1.4	0.7	8.8	2.5	16.3
Carmarthenshire	10.5	7.2	3.9	39.0	3.1	63.6
Ceredigion	7.2	5.0	2.7	44.1	2.3	61.2
Conwy	7.8	4.0	1.9	23.2	2.6	39.7
Denbighshire	7.1	3.7	1.7	20.7	2.9	36.0
Flintshire	4.4	2.1	1.1	10.9	2.9	21.4
Gwynedd	5.9	5.8	2.3	60.6	1.5	76.1
Merthyr Tydfil	4.0	1.7	1.0	7.4	3.7	17.7
Monmouthshire	2.1	1.6	0.6	6.8	1.8	12.9
Neath/Port Talbot	6.5	3.3	1.7	12.8	4.5	28.8
Newport	1.9	1.8	0.6	7.2	1.9	13.4
Pembrokeshire	5.4	3.5	1.6	16.4	2.4	29.4
Powys	6.1	3.2	1.7	16.0	3.2	30.1
Rhondda Cynon Taf	4.3	1.7	0.8	9.8	4.6	21.1
Swansea	6.0	2.5	1.4	9.4	3.3	22.5
Torfaen	1.9	1.9	0.7	8.1	1.8	14.5
Vale of Glamorgan	2.9	1.6	0.7	8.8	2.9	16.9
Wrexham	5.3	2.4	1.2	10.9	3.2	22.9
Ynys Môn	8.7	6.4	2.9	50.5	1.8	70.4
Wales	**4.9**	**2.8**	**1.4**	**16.3**	**3.0**	**28.4**

Table 3

Census Language Categories

As a Percentage of Population Aged 3 and Over with a Knowledge of Welsh : 2001

Local AuthorityArea	Understands Spoken Welsh only	Speaks Welsh, but does not read or write Welsh	Speaks and reads Welsh, but does not write Welsh	Speaks, reads and writes Welsh	Other comb- inations of skills
Blaenau Gwent	16.4	14.3	4.5	49.3	15.5
Bridgend	21.5	8.1	4.4	40.6	25.4
Caerphilly	17.0	10.3	4.0	51.1	17.6
Cardiff	18.0	8.6	4.3	53.7	15.5
Carmarthenshire	16.4	11.4	6.1	61.3	4.8
Ceredigion	11.7	8.1	4.5	72.0	3.7
Conwy	19.8	10.2	4.9	58.6	6.6
Denbighshire	19.6	10.2	4.8	57.5	7.9
Flintshire	20.5	10.0	5.0	51.1	13.5
Gwynedd	7.8	7.6	3.0	79.7	2.0
Merthyr Tydfil	22.7	9.7	5.5	41.4	20.8
Monmouthshire	16.0	12.5	4.6	53.1	13.9
Neath/Port Talbot	22.6	11.3	5.9	44.5	15.7
Newport	14.1	13.3	4.6	53.7	14.4
Pembrokeshire	18.5	12.0	5.6	55.7	8.3
Powys	20.2	10.6	5.6	53.1	10.6
Rhondda Cynon Taf	20.2	7.9	4.0	46.4	21.6
Swansea	26.7	11.0	6.1	41.7	14.5
Torfaen	13.4	13.3	4.8	55.9	12.7
Vale of Glamorgan	17.3	9.3	4.1	52.1	17.3
Wrexham	23.2	10.3	5.1	47.6	13.8
Ynys Môn	12.4	9.1	4.2	71.8	2.6
Wales	**17.4**	**9.9**	**4.8**	**57.4**	**10.5**

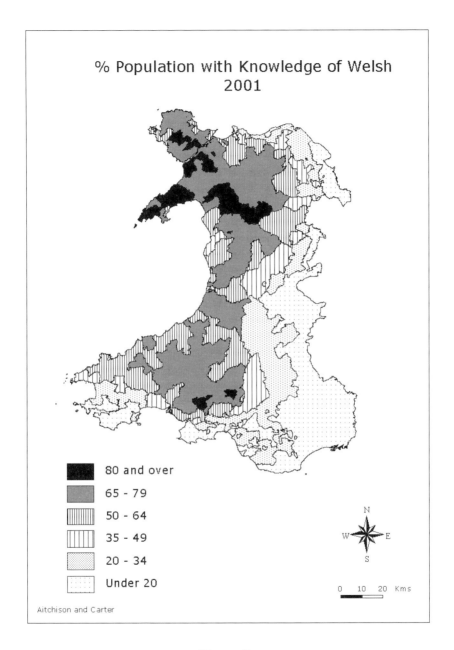

% Population with Knowledge of Welsh
2001

80 and over
65 - 79
50 - 64
35 - 49
20 - 34
Under 20

Aitchison and Carter

Figure 2.

41

Table 4

Knowledge of Welsh : Wards

Percentage of Population Aged 3 and Over

% Population with Knowledge of Welsh	Number of Wards	% Wards
Under 20	373	42.3
20-34	203	23.0
35-49	51	5.8
50-64	93	10.6
65-79	114	12.9
80 and over	47	5.3

in eastern Powys (e.g. Old Radnor, Llangunllo, Presteigne and Churchstoke).

While a description of variations in levels of knowledge of Welsh is of interest, offering an overview of linguistic strength, it is in itself a rather crude, general indicator. For deeper insights into the character of the linguistic landscape, a more detailed scrutiny of each of the five component language categories is needed.

Ability to Understand Spoken Welsh Only

As has already been indicated, the 2001 census included a new language item relating to the ability to 'understand' Welsh. In the statistical tabulations subsequently published by the Office for National Statistics this category refers specifically to those who could 'understand spoken Welsh only'. While information concerning an ability to 'understand' is commonly included in language surveys in other countries, its precise significance and meaning is difficult to ascertain. Thus, without further

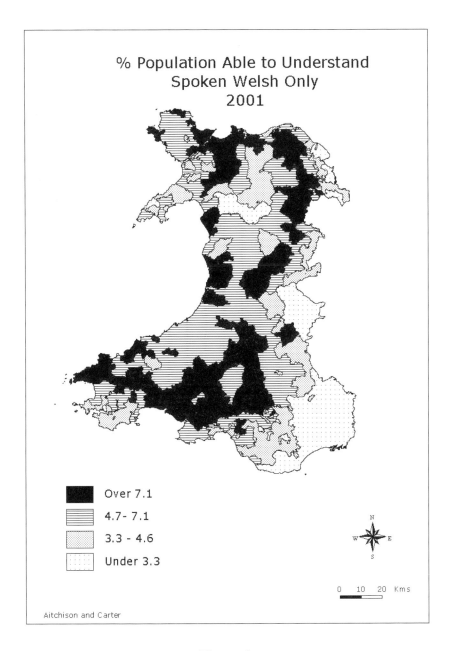

% Population Able to Understand
Spoken Welsh Only
2001

Over 7.1

4.7 - 7.1

3.3 - 4.6

Under 3.3

0   10   20   Kms

Aitchison and Carter

Figure 3.

43

background information it is impossible to determine whether or not the level of 'understanding' recorded within an area is a sign of language decline – a step in the process of language loss – or, alternatively, an intimation that the language is experiencing the first stages of further advancement. In the first case the persons concerned may simply have failed to progress beyond a basic appreciation of Welsh, possibly whilst living within a traditional Welsh-speaking community but where literacy standards have long been relatively low. Alternatively, they may indeed have 'unlearned' the language, as less and less use has been made of it. In the second case it may actually reflect a resurgence in the numbers of those who, possibly through local immersion, have come to 'understand' spoken Welsh, and who could well move on to acquire more advanced skills at a later date. Given that the census sheds no light on such matters all that can be attempted in seeking to interpret the published data is to relate them to their local contexts, and to reflect on possible implications for the future of the language in the areas concerned.

Of those enumerated in 2001, 138,416 claimed a sole ability to 'understand' spoken Welsh. They accounted for nearly 5 per cent of the total population aged 3 years and over, and 17.4 per cent of those with at least one skill in the language (i.e. with some knowledge of Welsh). In terms of geographical distribution the associated patterns are distinctive, but difficult to evaluate. In general, at local authority level, the highest percentages (in relation to the total population aged three and over) are recorded by areas situated within the traditional heartland of the Welsh language in the north and west (e.g. Carmarthenshire 10.5 per cent, Ynys Môn 8.7 per cent, Conwy 7.8 per cent and Ceredigion 7.2 per cent), but Gwynedd appears somewhat anomalous with a figure of just 5.9 per cent (Table 2). No doubt this is accounted for in part by the fact that over the years the region has succeeded in promoting very high levels of general literacy (see below). Broadly speaking, and adding weight to an argument broached above, it would seem that the highest proportions are to be found in areas where the incidence of Welsh-speaking is quite high, but where levels of literacy (i.e. abilities to read and write Welsh) are relatively low (e.g. Carmarthenshire and Conwy). Those local authorities with percentages of less than 3 are neatly clustered in the south-eastern quadrant of Wales – Cardiff 2.9 per cent, Caerphilly 2.8 per cent, Blaenau Gwent 2.2 per cent, Monmouthshire 2.1 per cent, Newport 1.9 per cent and Torfaen 1.9 per cent. An analysis of data for wards would suggest that locally the situation is in fact much more complex.

At ward level percentages of the population aged three and over with a sole ability to understand spoken Welsh range from a low of 0.9 to a high of 16.7, with an average 5.5. Figure 3 distinguishes four groups of divisions based on quartile thresholds and invites a number of observations. Firstly, it is worth noting (if only for the record) that in 2001 there was at least one person who could understand Welsh in each and every one of the wards of Wales – the language figured throughout the land! Secondly, low percentages (less than the lower quartile of 3.3) are largely confined to the south-east of Wales and eastern parts of the former district of Radnor. However, within the Welsh heartland a number of localities return equally low percentages – Llanrug (2.9 per cent), Penygroes (2.9 per cent), Llanuwchllyn (3.0 per cent), Tudweiliog (3.2 per cent) and Trawsfynydd (3.2 per cent). Thirdly, those areas recording the highest percentages – above the upper quartile of 7.1 per cent – define fragmented zones that encircle and penetrate the traditional Welsh core in north and mid Wales, whilst in south Wales they form an extensive band that extends from the Preseli Mountains in the west through the old industrial regions of Carmarthenshire and on into the Aman and Rhondda valleys. As far as the first of these two zones is concerned it might be argued that the high proportions bare testimony to the large numbers of incomers who over the years have gained a knowledge of Welsh, to the extent that they can understand the language spoken in an every day context. They have not, however, progressed further in terms of learning to speak, read or write Welsh. The areas concerned are the Vales of Conwy, Clwyd and Powys, and coastal parts of Ynys Môn, Meirionnydd and northern Ceredigion.

Interestingly, the highest percentages of all were returned by six wards in Ynys Môn – London Road, Porthyfelin, Parc a'r Mynydd, Morawelon, Maeshyfryd and Kingsland). Distinctively, these wards – each of which recorded a percentage in excess of 15 – form a singular cluster centred on the town of Holyhead. Even so, these areas are very closely associated with the fringes of the core which over the years have fallen away from being part of the 'Y Fro Gymraeg'. They may well represent a residual element of a once much stronger attachment to the language core via speech and literacy. It is thus possible to make two quite different interpretations of the data. But in the second of the two broad areas – south Wales – the situation would seem to be much simpler. Here the high percentages undoubtedly underline the general fragility of the language, a fragility that is confirmed by other data relating to literacy levels in these localities.

The discussion thus far has considered percentages based on the total population aged three and over. A somewhat different regional picture emerges, however, if the numbers of those able to understand spoken Welsh only are expressed as a percentage of the total number of persons with a declared knowledge of Welsh. Table 3 shows that for Wales as a whole the percentage figure is 17.4. Values in excess of 19.5 per cent are recorded by two distinct clusters of local authorities. They define two compact blocks; one in north and north-east Wales (Flintshire, Wrexham, Conwy and Denbighshire), and the other embracing local authorities in the western and central sections of the old industrial and coal-mining areas of south Wales – Swansea, Neath/Port Talbot, Rhondda Cynon Taf and Merthyr Tydfil. Powys also records a similarly high percentage. The lowest values – less than 15 per cent – are returned by the three mainly rural local authorities within the Welsh-speaking heartland – Gwynedd, Ynys Môn and Ceredigion. Interestingly, however, Torfaen on the outskirts of Cardiff returns an equally low percentage – 13.3. Figure 4 depicts the situation for wards. It re-affirms the broad patterns just described, but highlights certain local nuances. Thus, while most of the traditional rural heartland is indeed characterized by very low values – below the lower quartile of 14.9 per cent – within this zone the usual points of fracture or weakness are again discernable (e.g Conwy valley, coastal parts of Meirionnydd and northern Ceredigion). Here, percentages are seen to be somewhat higher. As in Figure 3, those areas with percentages in excess of the upper quartile are again to be found scattered throughout the borderland and along coastal parts of north Wales and south-west Wales. Particularly high values are recorded by wards within the areas of Swansea and Neath/Port Talbot. In these latter two authorities are located nine of the sixteen wards where percentages are 30 or over. It should be added that, on the basis of this measurement scale (i.e. with percentages based on the population with a knowledge of the language), wards in the urban and old industrial localities of south-east Carmarthenshire, and those across northern Pembrokeshire, do not stand out as strongly as they do in Figure 3.

Whilst the meaningfulness of the new language category is admittedly difficult to adjudge, it does offer a useful additional perspective in seeking to assess regional variations in the vitality of the language in Wales. The numbers involved – nearly 140,000 – are certainly not insignificant. That said, the question that needs to be asked is, does the sub-population of those who 'understand' the language constitute a robust base on which to build a more literate Welsh-speaking community (i.e. a body of language learners), or do they simply define a socio-linguistic grouping that has failed to move forward (or perhaps has even retreated), despite living and working within a strongly Welsh-speaking social environment? Disaggregating the data according to age and place of birth sheds little light on the matter. Nearly 40 per cent of those claiming an ability to understand spoken Welsh only are between 16 and 44 years of age, with a further 28 per cent being between 45 and 64. The percentages for those born in Wales and those born outside of Wales are 82 per cent and 18 per cent, respectively. Undoubtedly, it is possible that different explanations will be valid for different parts of Wales.

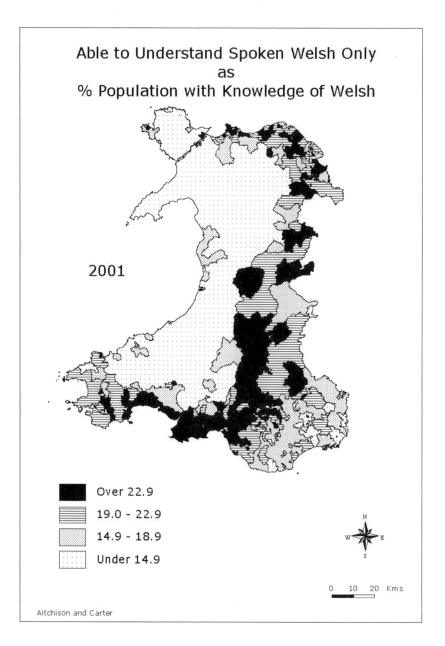

Able to Understand Spoken Welsh Only
as
% Population with Knowledge of Welsh

2001

Over 22.9

19.0 - 22.9

14.9 - 18.9

Under 14.9

N
W   E
S

0   10   20   Kms

Aitchison and Carter

Figure 4.

48

4. THE WELSH-SPEAKING POPULATION

This section of the discussion focuses on the Welsh-speaking population, and is accordingly much more detailed and wide-ranging in its treatment of the census data. In addition to examining the absolute and relative standing of the language in 2001, the analysis also explores the changes that have taken place between 1991 and 2001 in both the Welsh-speaking and non-Welsh-speaking populations. Other issues addressed include the distribution of Welsh-speakers in rural and urban areas, the age profiles of the Welsh-speaking community, employment attributes and levels of educational attainment.

(i) Distribution 2001

Of the various language categories distinguished in the census tabulations for 2001, it will be recalled that three specifically identify Welsh-speakers, differentiated according to literacy levels (i.e. abilities to speak, read and/or write Welsh). Aggregating these three categories yields a figure for the Welsh-speaking population in Wales of 575,640 – 20.5 per cent of those aged 3 and over (Table 5). These particular figures are derived from CAS tabulations. If reference is made to standard and theme tables, however, data are provided that directly record numbers of speakers, presumably including those speakers who were categorized in the 'other combinations of skills' category in the CAS tabulations. As to what the 'other combinations of skills' involving Welsh-speakers actually is or are it is difficult to imagine. Be that as it may, on this basis the Welsh-speaking population would appear to be somewhat higher at 582,368 – 20.8 per

Table 5

Population Aged 3 and over Able to Speak Welsh 1991 –2001*

Percentages, Percentage Differences and Rates of Change

Local Authority Area	Number Able to Speak Welsh	Number Able to Speak Welsh	% Able to Speak Welsh	% Able to Speak Welsh	% Differences	% Change
	1991	2001	1991	2001	1991-2001	1991-2001
Blaenau Gwent	1523	6141	2.2	9.1	6.9	303.2
Bridgend	10159	13155	8.2	10.6	2.4	29.5
Caerphilly	9714	17825	6.0	10.9	4.9	83.5
Cardiff	18080	31944	6.6	10.9	4.3	76.8
Carmarthenshire	89213	83802	54.8	50.1	-4.7	-6.1
Ceredigion	36026	37772	59.1	51.8	-7.3	4.8
Conwy	31443	31042	30.6	29.2	-1.4	-1.3
Denbighshire	23294	23540	26.7	26.1	-0.6	1.1
Flintshire	18399	20227	13.5	14.1	0.6	9.9
Gwynedd	78733	77495	72.1	68.7	-3.4	-1.6
Merthyr Tydfil	4237	5428	7.5	10.0	2.5	28.1
Monmouthshire	1631	7428	2.1	9.0	6.9	355.4
Neath/Port Talbot	23711	23182	17.8	17.8	0.0	2.2
Newport	2874	12608	2.3	9.6	7.3	338.7
Pembrokeshire	19759	23686	18.3	21.5	3.2	19.9
Powys	23590	25516	20.5	20.8	0.3	8.2
Rhondda Cynon Taf	20042	27505	9.0	12.3	3.3	37.2
Swansea	28557	28581	13.3	13.2	-0.1	0.1
Torfaen	2128	9425	2.5	10.7	8.2	342.9
Vale of Glamorgan	7755	12734	6.9	11.1	4.2	64.2
Wrexham	15990	17895	13.7	14.4	0.7	11.9
Ynys Môn	41240	38709	62.0	59.9	-2.2	-6.1
Wales	**508098**	**575640**	**18.7**	**20.5**	**1.8**	**13.3**

* Indicative only. Not adjusted for changes in boundaries or base populations

50

cent. Whilst it is important to draw attention to this particular calibration, in the discussion that follows it is to the CAS tabulations that reference is made since this allows a more refined evaluation of language structures, particularly in regards to literacy.

Whichever of the two figures for numbers of Welsh-speakers are cited, it is evident that historically they are of major symbolic significance, and confirm the predicted turning of the tide noted at the outset of this study. For the first time, since census enumerations were undertaken at the end of the nineteenth century, both the number and percentage of Welsh-speakers at national level show an inter-decennial increase. Indeed, the advance in absolute numbers of Welsh-speakers is such that the total now exceeds that recorded for the census of 1971 (542,425). Between 1991 and 2001 the numbers of Welsh-speakers increased by 13.3 per cent (14.6 per cent for the standard table data). The patterns of regional variation that underpin this momentous reversal of fortunes are considered later in the discussion.

In terms of the proportionate dominance of Welsh-speakers, data for local authorities (Table 5) affirm the continuing relative strength of the traditional heartland in the north and west. The emphasis here is on the word 'relative' for, as Table 5 shows, only in one area does the percentage of Welsh-speakers actually exceed 65 – Gwynedd (68.7 per cent). For the other main core regions – Ynys Môn, Ceredigion and Carmarthenshire the figures are just 59.9, 51.8 and 50.1, respectively. Such ratios clearly raise questions as to the longer term resilience of the language in these its supposed 'redoubts'. That said, beyond these regions the percentage dominance of Welsh-speakers is of a much lower order, with most authorities returning values of less than 25 per cent.

At ward level proportions of the respective populations able to speak Welsh vary greatly, from a minimum of 6.3 per cent for St Mary's (Monmouthshire) and St Thomas (Swansea) to a maximum of 88 per cent for Peblig (Gwynedd) and Penygroes (Gwynedd). The average

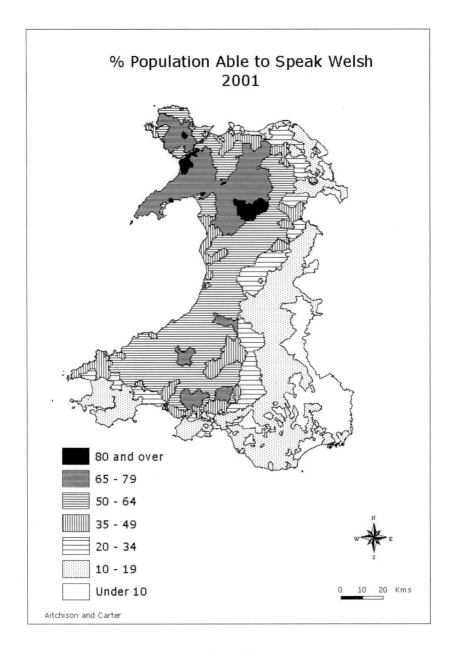

% Population Able to Speak Welsh
2001

80 and over
65 - 79
50 - 64
35 - 49
20 - 34
10 - 19
Under 10

Aitchison and Carter

0   10   20   Kms

Figure 5.

percentage for all wards stands at 26.6 per cent, with a median of 13.6 per cent. Table 6 shows that for 62.3 per cent (549) of wards, these proportions are less than 20. Together, they account for nearly 42 per cent (239, 814) of all Welsh-speakers. Less than 10 per cent of wards (85) have Welsh-speaking populations of 65 per cent or more. They have nearly 19 per cent of all Welsh-speakers. The tabulation highlights the fact that whilst there are some very strong clusters where Welsh-speakers are locally very dominant, these are relatively small in number. The great majority of Welsh-speakers are widely scattered and live in areas where percentages are still relatively low. This is well illustrated in Figure 5. The highest figures (over 80 per cent) are seen to be confined to a dispersed and very limited set of wards located in Gwynedd and Ynys Môn. One particularly prominent cluster of ten wards lies to the south of Caernarfon. The localities concerned are – Peblig/Caernarfon (88 per cent), Penygroes (88 per cent), Llanrug (87 per cent), Seiont (87 per cent), Groeslon (86 per cent), Cadnant (86 per cent), Bethel (86 per cent) Menai/Caernarfon (84 per cent), Bontnewydd (84 per cent) and Llanwnda (82 per cent). Within the rest of Gwynedd just four other divisions returned percentages of over 80 – Porthmadog East (84 per cent), Diffwys and Maenofferen (84 per cent), Pwllheli North (82 per cent) and Llanuwchllyn (81 per cent). On Ynys Môn only three areas around Llangefni recorded percentages of a similar order – Cyngar (84 per cent), Tudur (83 per cent) and Cefni (83 per cent). Together, all of these wards with the highest percentages of Welsh-speakers can be seen as the fragmented residuum of a once extensive and totally dominant area of Welsh speech, embracing Llŷn, the former districts of Arfon and Ynys Môn, together with Meirionnydd-Nant Conwy centred on Penllyn (Bala) and Blaenau Ffestiniog. A further telling feature of the distribution is that in 2001 no wards outside of Gwynedd and Ynys Môn recorded percentages of Welsh-speakers of 80 or more.

Areas with percentages between 60 and 79 extend across large parts of Gwynedd and Ynys Môn, as well as the western fringes of Denbighshire.

Table 6

Welsh-speaking Population : Wards

Percentage of Population Aged 3 and over Able to Speak Welsh : 2001

% Welsh-speakers	Number of Wards	Number of Welsh-speakers	% of All Welsh-speakers
Under 10	181	65719	11.4
10-19.9	368	174095	30.2
20-34.9	74	50929	8.9
35-49.9	67	64742	11.2
50-64.9	106	111733	19.4
65-79.9	68	84445	14.7
80 and over	17	23976	4.2

Only a small number of wards achieved similar proportions in mid and south Wales. Figure 5 reveals that for most of the traditional heartland region percentages of Welsh-speakers were disturbingly low – between 50 and 64. Included in this grouping are coastal wards on Ynys Môn, a wedge of wards that penetrates into the Snowdonia region in northern Gwynedd, together with wards extending across virtually the whole of Ceredigion and much of Carmartheshire. Fringing, and encroaching into, these areas are localities where Welsh-speakers no longer constitute the majority of the population. Here percentages are between 35 and 49. Worthy of attention are two distinctive clusters on the west coast of Wales. The one extends from St David's to Fishguard in north Pembrokeshire, the other from Aberystywth across the estuaries of the Dyfi and the Mawddach to Dyffryn Ardudwy. A similar, but much smaller, cluster is formed by the two wards centred on Abersoch and Llanbedrog in the Llŷn Peninsula. The attraction of each of these regions for tourists, second-home owners and the retired continues to profoundly influence their social and cultural character.

Figure 5 also indicates that a sharp discontinuity defines the divide between a predominantly Welsh-speaking region and an overwhelmingly Anglicized periphery. Wards with percentages of Welsh-speakers ranging between 20 and 34 are limited in number and form a long, narrow band along the eastern edge of the main heartland region. Throughout much of the borderland, the Vale of Glamorgan, the Gower Peninsula, and southern and central parts of Pembrokeshire, percentages of Welsh-speakers are less than 20. Values of less than 10 are mainly confined to Monmouthshire, the former mining valleys of Blaenau Gwent and Caerphilly, Newport, and the eastern fringes of Brecknock and Radnor.

While the proportionate dominance of Welsh-speakers serves as a proxy measure of the degree of social communication that might take place through the medium of Welsh at a local level, and is accordingly the measure most frequently used in distinguishing regional variations in the strength of the language, it is evident that to complete the picture reference also needs to be made to absolute numbers of Welsh-speakers. As Figure 6 shows, plotting actual numbers of speakers offers an alternative insight into the geography of the language. In assessing this particular distribution it is important to appreciate that the proportionate circles, which categorize wards on the basis of numbers of speakers, are located not at the spatial centre of gravity of the areas concerned, but at their demographic centre (i.e. the spatial centre weighted according the distribution of population). The resultant pattern is revealing. A notable feature is the relative emptiness of much of what is traditionally regarded as the Welsh-speaking heartland. This is especially the case in north Wales. Here, most of the Welsh-speakers are seen to be clustered around coastal margins, and with a particularly dominant concentration being highlighted in the Bangor-Caernarfon region. In the former district of Meirionnydd numbers are very thin on the ground. Further south, in Ceredigion, the Welsh-speaking community has a stronger numerical presence, most especially along the coast and within the Teifi valley. By far the greatest numbers of Welsh-speakers, however, are seen to be located in the urban and industrial centres of south Wales. Two linked strings of wards stand out in particular. The one extends from Kidwelly, through Pontyberem, Ammanford and Gwaun-Cae-Gurwen to Ystradgynlais. The other follows the line of the Tawe valley, from Ystalyfera through Pontardawe and Clydach to Swansea; from there it stretches westwards to encompass the towns of Gorseinon and Llanelli. Together, these two dominant clusters account for just over 100,000 Welsh-speakers. A further very strong concentration identified in Figure 6 is that centred on the capital city of Cardiff. Here just over 30,000 Welsh-speakers were enumerated. Less strong, but still worthy of note, is the tightly grouped collection of wards in the Newport area. As for the valleys of the former coalfield region these are well delineated, and collectively they account for fairly substantial numbers of speakers. Finally, it is evident that throughout the borderland numbers of Welsh-speakers are very low, apart from certain urban areas in north-east Wales (e.g. the Chirk, Ruabon, Rhosllanerchrugog, Wrexham axis, and around Mold).

The distribution of numbers of Welsh-speakers depicted in Figure 6 draws attention to the critical importance of urban environments for the reproduction of the language. It also serves to underline the fact that while it is customary to identify the Welsh-speaking community with rural areas of north and west Wales (*Y Fro Gymraeg*), the actual heartland of that community in terms of absolute numbers lies in south Wales, embracing the long-standing Welsh-speaking communities of the former western coal-field and the burgeoning regions to the east, with Cardiff as a powerful focal point. These matters are considered again below in an analysis of the language in rural and urban contexts.

For purposes of reference, the number and percentage of Welsh-speakers in each of the 881 wards are detailed in an Appendix at the end of this text.

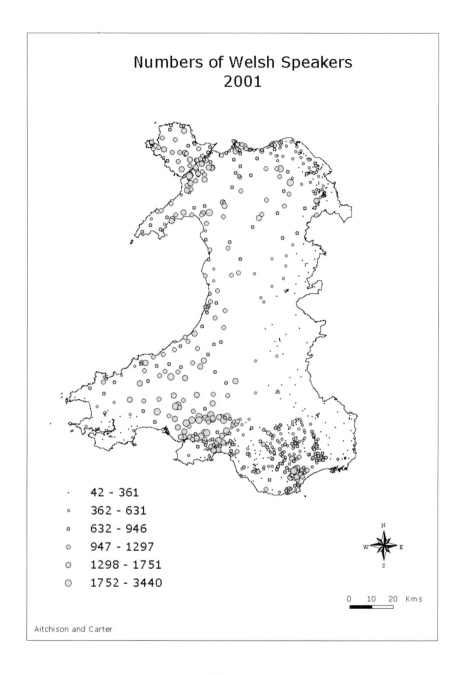

Numbers of Welsh Speakers
2001

- 42 - 361
- 362 - 631
- 632 - 946
- 947 - 1297
- 1298 - 1751
- 1752 - 3440

Aitchison and Carter

Figure 6.

While the relative and absolute strength of the Welsh-speaking community, as depicted in Figures 5 and 6, repeats in very broad terms the patterns of distribution evident in the 1991 census (see Aitchison and Carter, 2000), it is apparent that over the intervening decade changes of some significance have occurred. It is to the assessment of these changes that the discussion now turns. Before so doing, however, it is necessary to consider some of the technical complexities involved in seeking to quantify the magnitude and direction of these changes.

(ii) Change 1991–2001

As has already been noted, changes to the boundaries of administrative areas, together with differences in the definition of base populations, make the precise measurement of language change for the period 1991–2001 particularly difficult. The issue of the base population, it will be recalled, relates in particular to the enumeration in 2001 of students at their term-time addresses, rather than at their usual home addresses, as was the case for the 1991 census. Unfortunately, this is a matter that cannot be statistically circumvented with any degree of accuracy. As a result any discussion of change in, for example, numbers of Welsh-speakers, needs to be qualified with due recognition of the necessary caveats. This certainly applies for those localities, such as university towns, that are likely to be the most heavily affected, but it has implications for all areas. A gain in numbers of students for some regions implies a loss for others (*ceteris paribus*).

The boundary problem can be more readily addressed, but requires a careful re-grouping of areas to arrive at a common spatial frame for the years concerned. For this study the boundaries of wards for 1991 have been matched against those for 2001 using a Geographical Information System (ArcView). Technically, this involves the overlaying of so-called "shape" files to ascertain common boundary segments and deviations. Taking the wards for 2001 as the standard frame of reference, a new set of areas has been created. This set comprises single wards, the boundaries of which are the same as those in 1991; individual wards, the 2001 boundaries of which precisely match two or more areas in 1991; and groupings of 2001 wards, the collective boundaries of which can be aligned with those of one or more 1991 wards. This re-structuring process has been undertaken to ensure that the new areas identified are as small as they possibly can be. For these new areas the total numbers of Welsh-speakers have been determined for 1991 and 2001.

The new set of wards derived here, henceforth referred to as the 'standard set', comprises 764 'ward areas'. Adopting the procedure outlined above, these areas were established through the matching of the 881 wards for the 2001 census with the 908 for the 1991 census. Since the process involved in creating the standard set is unavoidably one of aggregation rather than sub-division, it is inevitable that there will be a loss of some spatial detail. Obviously, this is particularly the case in areas where local authorities radically altered the alignment of administrative boundaries between 1991 and 2001.

Having established a standard frame of reference it is possible to proceed to the measurement of change in proportions and numbers of Welsh-speakers, and to consider how these changes relate to associated movements in total populations for the areas concerned. As in previous studies, it is appropriate to consider differences in percentages (i.e. for each ward area the percentage of the population aged 3 and over able to speak Welsh in 2001 minus the equivalent figure for 1991), and rates of change in numbers of speakers (i.e. increases or decreases in numbers of Welsh-speakers, expressed in percentage terms).

(a) Differences in Percentages

Table 5 shows that for each of the four local authority areas generally regarded as constituting the traditional Welsh-speaking heartland – Gwynedd, Ynys Môn, Ceredigion and Carmarthenshire – the percentages of their respective populations (aged 3 and over) able to speak Welsh fell

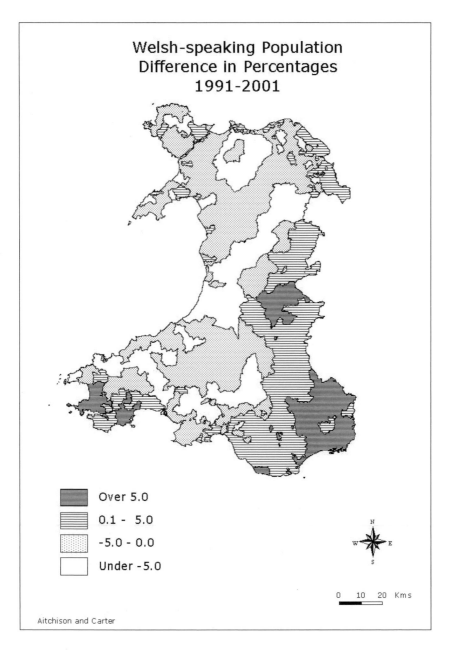

Welsh-speaking Population
Difference in Percentages
1991-2001

Over 5.0

0.1 - 5.0

-5.0 - 0.0

Under -5.0

N
W E
S

0   10   20   Kms

Aitchison and Carter

Figure 7.

Table 7

Differences in Percentages of Welsh-speakers 1991-2001

| | Percentage Differences | | | |
| | Negative | | Positive | |
	<-5.0	-5.0 to 0.0	0.1 to 5.0	> 5.0
Number of Ward Areas	103	197	318	146
Number of Welsh-speakers 1991	130171	218380	138819	21014
Number of Welsh-speakers 2001	120759	210608	181016	63256
% of All Welsh-speakers 1991	25.6	42.9	27.3	4.1
% All Welsh-speakers 2001	21.0	36.6	31.4	11.0

between 1991 and 2001 (Table 5). The fall was especially marked in the case of Ceredigion (-7.3 per cent). Negative, but more limited, differences applied in only three other areas – Conwy, Denbighshire and Swansea. As far as increases in percentage values are concerned, these were widely recorded, with strong advances being returned for Torfaen (8.2 per cent), Newport (7.3 per cent), Blaenau Gwent (6.9 per cent), Monmouthshire (6.9 per cent), Caerphilly (4.9 per cent) and Cardiff (4.3 per cent).

A more detailed insight into regional variations is provided by Figure 7 which charts differences in percentages for the standard set of wards, with areas being classified into four basic groupings. Table 7 details the total number of Welsh-speakers within each of these groupings, together with associated percentages. The resultant patterns are very revealing, and highlight significant regional differences. Critically for the future of the language, the 103 ward areas recording negative differences in percentages of more than 5 (the strongest levels of decline) are seen to be dominantly located within *Y Fro Gymraeg*. Particularly noteworthy are: clusters of wards stretching across the hills and uplands between Betws-y-Coed in

Snowdonia to Llansannan on the northern fringes of Mynydd Hiraethog; a dispersed collection of areas in the Llŷn Peninsula and on Ynys Môn; a long line of wards stretching at an angle across mid-Wales from Newquay on the Ceredigion coast to the border with England to the south of Oswestry (Llandrinio); a fragmented, arcuate band of areas that extends across northern parts of Pembrokeshire, through into the old industrial regions centred on Pontyberem and Ammanford, and on into the area encompassing the Black Mountain. In 1991 the 103 areas within this category of highest decline were home to just over a quarter of Welsh-speakers, but by 2001 this proportion had fallen to 21 per cent. Table 7 also indicates that collectively these same areas recorded a loss of more than 9,000 speakers between 1991 and 2001.

Figure 7 also reveals that surrounding these localities recording the sharpest falls are a large number of ward areas (197) where decline is still in evidence, although to a lesser degree. The areas within this grouping recorded differences in percentages ranging from -5 to 0. Once again they are largely confined to the traditional heartland. This particular grouping returned the greatest number of Welsh-speakers in 2001 (210, 608), but the total was nearly 8,000 down on that for 1991. The areas concerned claimed 42.9 per cent of all Welsh-speakers in 1991, but by 2001 the figure had fallen to 36.6 per cent. Together, all those wards showing negative differences (i.e. the two groups that have just been described) accounted for 68.5 per cent of all Welsh-speakers in 1991. By 2001 this had declined quite dramatically to just 57.7 per cent. The once so dominant bastions of the language are seen to be weakening in both absolute and relative terms. It follows from this that the national advance in the number of Welsh-speakers has taken place beyond the traditional core areas – along the borderland and across the strongly Anglicized lowland regions of south Wales.

Figure 7 confirms that the highest increases in percentages (above 5 per cent) were recorded by wards throughout much of Monmouthshire, in the local authorities of Blaenau Gwent, Caerphilly and Newport, in parts of Cardiff, and across much of south Pembrokeshire. Within the borderland a notable cluster to the north of Llandrindod Wells (e.g. Nantmel and Beguildy) returned similar advances. Eleven areas, mostly located in south-east Wales, achieved increases in excess of 9 per cent. In 2001 the 146 ward areas that recorded rises of more than 5 per cent accounted for 11 per cent of all Welsh-speakers; in 1991 the same areas contained just 4 per cent (Table 7). The remaining ward areas, yielding smaller but still positive values (i.e. those with percentage differences between 0.1 and 5.0), extend across large parts of south Wales (including the former coal-mining valleys), throughout much of eastern Powys and Flintshire, and along the north coast of Wales. Within the traditional heartland of the language only a small number of areas saw positive advances in percentages of this particular order. These exceptions include Llanystumdwy and Nefyn in the Llŷn Pensinsula, Porthmadog West, a cluster of areas in the region between Menai Bridge and Benllech on Ynys Môn, and an isolated set of wards along the coast of Meirionnydd – Tywyn and Barmouth. These are difficult to explain, and can perhaps best be viewed as areas that, for the time being, had escaped (in pure numerical terms and according to the thresholds specified) the changes that had affected the larger area which surrounds them. In 2001 over 31 per cent of all Welsh-speakers were resident in areas that recorded modest increases in percentages between 1991 and 2001. The equivalent figure for 1991 was 27 per cent (Table 7).

This analysis of differences in percentages confirms the relative weakening of the Welsh language within its stronghold areas, and the emergence of Anglo-Wales as a zone of linguistic expansion. The expansion in this latter zone is noteworthy, but it has to be said that it is an advance from a very low base. While an assessment of differences in percentages is highly revealing in its own right, and critically important to any evaluation of the maintenance and reproduction of the language, it is evident that

63

the strength and direction of such differences depends both on the rate and direction of change in numbers of Welsh-speakers and on changes in the sizes of resident populations. It is these particular changes that now need to be considered.

(b) Rates of Change

Table 5 records percentage rates of change in absolute numbers of Welsh-speakers at local authority level for the period 1991 and 2001. Although based on the assumption that the two census enumerations are directly comparable, which very strictly speaking they are not, the resultant statistics can be viewed as broadly indicative of prevailing trends. They indicate that in three of the four core Welsh-speaking areas numbers of Welsh-speakers actually declined – Carmarthenshire (-6.1 per cent), Ynys Môn (-6.1 per cent) and Gwynedd (-1.6 per cent). Ceredigion is anomalous, however, in that an increase of 4.8 per cent in absolute numbers was recorded (even though the proportion of speakers declined – see above). Without more detailed data on the possible impact of the student population and general migration trends it difficult to account for this particular regional difference. Overall, within the heartland the situation is as predicted – a decline in both the absolute and relative strength of the language.

Elsewhere in Wales, the picture is one of a general increase in numbers of speakers. Although admittedly starting from low bases, the surges highlighted in Monmouthshire (355 per cent), Torfaen (343 per cent), Newport (339 per cent) and Blaenau Gwent (303 per cent) serve to underscore the emergence of south-east Wales as a major growth area for the language. Other local authority areas returning strong increases are Caerphilly (83 per cent), Cardiff (77 per cent), Vale of Glamorgan (64 per cent) and Rhondda Cynon Taf (37 per cent). Together, these eight regions recorded just over 125,000 Welsh-speakers; this amounts to nearly 22 per cent of the total for the whole of Wales. While the proportion of the population speaking Welsh in these areas is still low in relative terms, it is evident that the actual numbers involved are considerable (see Figure 6). They contribute significantly to the pool of speakers in Wales; indeed they underpin the very revival in the fortunes of the language at national level (at least in crude quantitative terms). As expected, the growth in these areas has more than compensated for the decline in numbers of speakers elsewhere, and their contribution is likely to be even greater in the years to come. The linguistic centre of gravity in Wales is slowly shifting, and much has already been said as to the factors involved. More than anything else it is the promotion of the language in schools and centres of higher education that is responsible for the rejuvenation of the language in these areas of rapid growth. The youthfulness of the Welsh-speaking population in the regions of Anglo-Wales is examined later.

Figure 8 categorizes the standard set of ward areas according to the percentage rate of change in numbers of Welsh-speakers. The highest rates of decline (i.e. falls in excess of 10 per cent) are seen to be recorded by a dispersed collection of areas (88), mainly located within and on the fringes of the traditional heartland. Included in this category is a large, contiguous cluster extending from eastern Snowdonia and the Conwy Valley into northern and central parts of Mynydd Hiraethog; areas in the Llŷn Peninsula (i.e. Tudweiliog and Clynnog), on Ynys Môn (e.g. Amlwch and Aberffraw), in Meirionnydd (Llanuwchllyn) and Powys (Glantwymyn/ Llanbrynmair); an extensive sweep of wards centred on Ystradgynlais, Pontardawe and Pontardulais in south Wales, and a group of six areas stretching from St David's to Newport along the northern coast of Pembrokeshire. Table 8 shows that the ward areas within this grouping accounted for nearly 19 per cent of all Welsh-speakers in 1991, but that by 2001 this had fallen to 14.0 per cent. A decline in numbers of Welsh-speakers also characterizes a large number of other areas (138), although here the rate is more muted (between -10.0 per cent and 0 per cent). The wards concerned dominate in much of Gwynedd (including the Llŷn

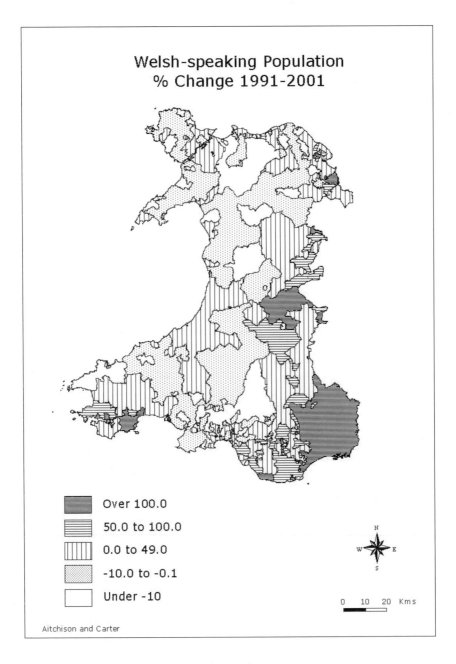

Welsh-speaking Population
% Change 1991-2001

Legend:
- Over 100.0
- 50.0 to 100.0
- 0.0 to 49.0
- -10.0 to -0.1
- Under -10

0   10   20   Kms

Aitchison and Carter

Figure 8.

Table 8

Percentage Rates of Change in Numbers of Welsh-speakers 1991-2001

	Negative		Positive		
	<-10%	-10% to 0%	0.1% to 49%	50% to 100%	>100%
Number of Ward Areas	88	138	293	107	138
Number of Welsh-speakers 1991	95428	171807	189450	34127	17572
Number of Welsh-speakers 2001	80708	163435	214265	57852	59379
% All Welsh-speakers 1991	18.8	33.8	37.3	6.7	3.5
% All Welsh-speakers 2001	14.0	28.4	37.2	10.1	10.3

Peninsula), in Ynys Môn, and in northern Carmarthenshire. In 1991 33.8 per cent of all Welsh-speakers were resident within these regions; by 2001 this proportion had decreased to just 28.4 per cent. As in the analysis of differences in percentages it is evident that ward areas recording a reduction in numbers of Welsh-speakers are largely confined to the traditional heartland. Within this broad area there are, however, some notable local variations where numbers of speakers have increased.

Figure 8 and Table 8 differentiate three categories for ward areas recording positive rates of change between 1991 and 2001. The largest of these distinguishes those areas – 293 in total – where numbers of Welsh-speakers have increased by between 0.1 and 49 per cent. Included in this grouping are wards that cover much of Ceredigion, central Pembrokeshire and Carmarthenshire, northern and southern sections of Powys, Flintshire, Wrexham and eastern parts of Denbighshire. Similar rates of increase are also seen to apply in the region between, and inland from, Caernarfon and Bangor in Gwynedd, and across the Menai Straits around Beaumaris and Menai Bridge. The category identifying ward areas where numbers of speakers have increased by between 50 per cent and 100 per cent are mainly confined to the Vale of Glamorgan, south-western parts of Pembrokeshire, central Brecknock and the eastern fringes of Montgomeryshire. As for those localities recording the highest increases of all (in excess of 100 per cent), they define a compact region encompassing virtually the whole of Monmouthshire and Newport, and parts of Blaenau Gwent, Caerphilly and Cardiff. Elsewhere equally high increases apply in areas around Tenby, and to the north of Llandrindod Wells in Powys. In regards to the very high increases returned in these regions (for example, 26 areas recorded increases in excess of 500 per cent), it has to be said again that they derive mainly from low initial bases (i.e. low numbers of speakers in 1991), and that the subsequent rise in numbers of Welsh-speakers by 2001 is largely accounted for by the teaching of Welsh within the schools of the areas concerned. This raises questions as to the precise significance of the recorded advance, and in particular its capacity to consolidate given the broader social context in which it is taking place. Be that as it may, Table 8 indicates that, together, those ward areas where rates of change were positive claimed nearly 58 per cent of the Welsh-speaking population in 2001. In 1991 the equivalent figure was 47.5 per cent – such had been the pace of expansion over the decade.

(c) Language Change Categories

While separate analyses of differences in percentages and percentage rates of change yield differing insights and perspectives on linguistic trends, it is helpful to consider the two measures in integrated fashion – albeit in a very simplified manner. To this end Figure 9 classifies ward areas according to the direction of change on each of the measures (i.e. positive or negative). Four categories are therefore identified. The largest category in terms of numbers of wards (Category 1) distinguishes the most dynamic areas as far as language trends are concerned, for it includes those areas (451) where both the percentage and number of persons able to speak Welsh increased between 1991 and 2001. In terms of their distribution several distinct regions can be discerned. Firstly, an extensive and compact zone can be identified encompassing the eastern borderland fringes of Montgomeryshire, much of Radnor and Brecknock, Monmouthshire, Cardiff and Newport, the Vale of Glamorgan, parts of Swansea, and local authorities within the old coal-mining valleys of south Wales. Separated from this large area, but essentially an extension of it, is a cluster of areas in Flintshire and Wrexham. A further strongly-defined region encompasses the whole of south and central Pembrokeshire. Another interesting feature is the string of wards located along the coast of North Wales, from Prestatyn to Llandudno. Elsewhere a number of individual wards have similar language profiles – Tywyn, Barmouth, Porthmadog West, Nefyn and Llanwnda in Gwynedd, and Beaumaris, Pentraeth, Llanbedrgoch and Llanfair-yn-Neubwll on Ynys Môn. Together, the 451 areas that fall within this strong growth category had a combined Welsh-speaking population of 233,946 in 2001 – some 41 per cent of the total for Wales. This compares with a total of just 149,310 in 1991 – an increase of nearly 57 per cent.

The second largest of the four trend categories (category 4 in Figure 9) comprises 213 ward areas. Here the defining attribute is one of decline on all fronts – between 1991 and 2001 percentages of Welsh-speakers fell and numbers declined. The downturn was both relative and absolute. Figure 9 shows that the areas concerned extend across a major part of Wales and, as would be expected given the above discussions, define a zone that largely accords with that of the Welsh-speaking heartland. In north Wales it includes the greater part of Ynys Môn, Gwynedd and Denbighshire. Further to the south the picture is more complicated, but the distribution distinguishes areas of wholesale decline in northern Pembrokeshire, parts of Ceredigion (e.g. Tregaron, Lledrod, the lower Teifi valley), central and eastern parts of Carmarthenshire, the boroughs of Swansea, Neath and the Rhondda, and parts of south-western Powys. In 1991 the wards within this grouping recorded a Welsh-speaking population of 256,532 – 50 per cent of all Welsh-speakers. By 2001 the number of speakers in these same areas had fallen to 233,817 – 40 per cent of the total Welsh-speaking population.

A particularly distinctive grouping (Category 2 in Figure 9) comprises 87 ward areas where numbers of Welsh-speakers increased but associated percentages actually decreased – a situation of absolute advance accompanied by relative decline. These areas are widely dispersed across Wales, but some notable clusters are highlighted. The first extends across much of Ceredigion, with an extension southwards into Carmarthenshire between Llanfihangel-ar-arth and the area to the west of Llandeilo. The second encompasses the region to the south of Mynydd Preseli between St Clears and Haverfordwest. A third compact cluster stretches across the hill areas around Lake Vyrnwy to the west of the settlements of Llanfair Caereinion and Llanfyllin (Powys). In north Wales two further regions stand out – the one follows the line of the Vale of Clwyd, the other lies along the coast and inland from Caernarfon and Bangor, and covers much of the Snowdonia massif. In 1991 the areas within this particular grouping had a Welsh-speaking population of 92,019; by 2001 this had increased by 6 per cent to 97,550.

The final group (Category 3) identified in Figure 9 comprises just 13 ward areas. Here numbers of Welsh-speakers declined between 1991 and 2001, but in proportionate terms they increased. The localities concerned are again dispersed in distribution, but with the majority being located in the local authority regions of Brigend and Neath. Two wards in north Wales are worth noting, however – Llanystumdwy in the Llŷn Peninsula, and Cwm Cadnant (between Menai Bridge and Beaumaris) on Ynys Môn. The Welsh-speaking population in the 13 wards was 10,703 in 1991, and 10,326 in 2001.

At this point, and before moving on to compare patterns of change among Welsh-speaking and non-Welsh-speaking populations, it is appropriate to focus briefly on the language situation within a symbolically

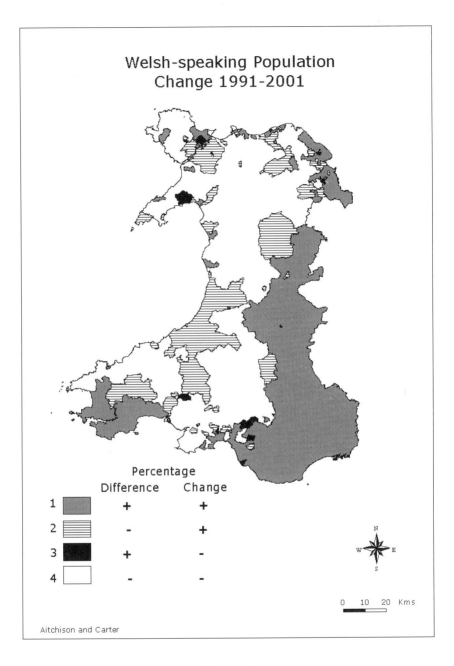

Welsh-speaking Population
Change 1991-2001

Percentage

		Difference	Change
1		+	+
2		-	+
3		+	-
4		-	-

0   10   20   Kms

Aitchison and Carter

Figure 9.

71

significant region – the city of Cardiff. In previous studies, based on census data for 1971 and 1981 and on questionnaire surveys of children in primary and secondary schools, the authors described the developments in Cardiff and its immediate hinterland as a 'quiet revolution', and one that could have profound consequences for the future of the language nationally (Aitchison and Carter, 1985). In the once overwhelmingly Anglicized capital city Welsh was seen to be increasingly associated with an emerging professional class, working in the media, education, financial institutions and the public services. The language gained in status and an ability to speak Welsh was '*recherché*' – a defining cultural attribute to be studiously cultivated or sought after. Its position within the social fabric was further consolidated by young, upwardly mobile couples with children who successfully engineered the expansion of educational provision through the medium of Welsh. Thus, here, in an urban environment far removed from the isolated rural villages and farms of '*Y Fro Gymraeg*' the language was given a new lease of life. In their earlier studies, however, Aitchison and Carter raised doubts as to how deeply-rooted and expansive these developments would prove to be in a cosmopolitan and highly dynamic environment. Given this, it is of interest to consider whether or not the trends previously identified in this key region were maintained for the period 1991–2001.

Before so doing, however, some technical problems need to be mentioned. Boundary changes, both to the city limits and, internally, to the alignment of particular wards mean that adjustments have to be made to the basic census dataset before analysis can proceed. The city limits were extended to incorporate areas formerly within the district of Taff-Ely (in particular the wards of Creigiau and Pentyrch), and the ward of Radyr and St Fagans (as it was in 1991) was also radically altered in its layout. All other changes can be accommodated through aggregation, but not so some modifications made to the boundaries of certain wards on the western edge of the city (i.e. Caerau and Ely). These, however, are of a minor order and do not greatly affect the accuracy of the analysis. The resultant frame comprises 27 ward areas set within the city limits, as defined at the 2001 census (Table 9). One further point, in considering the data for Cardiff with its substantial centres of higher education it is again necessary to emphasize that the differential treatment of students at the two censuses complicates analysis, and cannot be circumvented. All that can be said is that while the 2001 figures will contain many young Welsh-speakers who had temporarily moved into the city for their studies, those for 1991 included Welsh-speakers who were not actually resident in Cardiff at the time of the enumeration (i.e. were based at centres of study, either elsewhere in Wales or beyond its borders). As far as the numbers of Welsh-speakers are concerned, therefore, there are indeterminate losses and gains for each of the censuses.

In 2001 the total Welsh-speaking population enumerated in Cardiff was 31,944; in 1991 it was 18,071. This is a very substantial increase of nearly 77 per cent. In 1991 Welsh-speakers accounted for 6.6 per cent of the population aged 3 years and over, by 2001 this had increased to 10.9. Writing of the 1981 pattern the authors emphasized the association of Welsh-speakers in the city with the higher class residential areas. They maintained that the distribution was 'largely sectoral in structure, with three dominant zones of above average percentages... extending out from the city centre and ultimately coalescing in the suburban... periphery. The first and most evident of these sectors or wedges runs westward through Llandaff to Radyr and St Fagans. The other two sectors... are more fragmented in form and have a common focus in the south-east of the city at Roath. From there one band... reaches north-westwards to Llanishen and Rhiwbina, whilst the other strikes north through Pen-y-lan... to Lisvane' (Aitchison and Carter, 2000, 78–82). Sharp breaks between these sectors were formed by Tongwynlais in the north-west, at Ely in the south-west and St Mellons in the east. The statistics collated in Table 9 would suggest that broadly-speaking these sectors were still apparent in 2001. The sector including Llandaff (15.2 per cent) and Creigiau-St Fagans-Radyr (16.4 per cent) is still a prominent feature, and indeed has been extended further with the addition of Pentyrch. This latter ward actually returned the highest proportion of Welsh-speakers in the city – 18.6 per cent (Table 9) Again, Llanishen (11.0 per cent) and Rhiwbina (12.6 per cent) returned percentages higher than the average for the city. The third sector is not as evident, although Cyncoed recorded an above average figure of 11.5 per cent.

While the sectoral structure would appear to have remained intact, closer scrutiny of the data draws attention to other interesting developments. Of particular note are those wards recording increases in numbers of Welsh-speakers of more than 100 per cent. Significantly, these include areas such as Splott, Butetown, Grangetown, Trowbridge, Llanrumney, Gabalfa, Rumney and Ely (Table 9) where proportions of the population able to speak Welsh were particularly low in 1991. They were still relatively low in 2001, but there can be no doubting the advances made over the decade. It is difficult to account for the changes that have taken place in these areas without further detailed investigation. Interpretation is made all the more problematic by the inclusion in the census returns of students who dominate the rooming-house areas about the city centre, and by the impact that the new residential developments at Cardiff Bay have had on social structures. Whatever the reasons, the data would suggest that the Welsh-speaking community in Cardiff is both expanding, and becoming more widely-spread across the city. All of the wards exhibiting high levels of growth lie outside of the strong Welsh-speaking sectors previously identified. These trends, if they were to continue, would be noteworthy and could herald the incipient development of a broader bilingualism. The sign is indeed 'a little cloud… no bigger than a man's hand', but it could mark the start of something much more significant.

Table 9

Cardiff : Welsh Language Statistics 1991–2001

WardAreas	Number of Welsh-speakers 2001	% Population Welsh-speaking 2001	% Change in Welsh-speaking Population 1991–2001	Differences in Welsh-speaking Percentages 1991–2001
Adamsdown	591	8.9	91.3	4.5
Butetown	358	8.3	222.5	5.2
Caerau	876	9.0	113.1	4.8
Canton	1941	15.4	88.4	7.3
Cathays	1330	9.7	116.3	3.2
Creigiau/St. Fagans/Radyr★	1403	16.4	41.4	-2.3
Cyncoed	1156	11.5	23.9	2.3
Ely	1342	9.6	123.3	5.5
Fairwater	1090	9.1	87.9	4.4
Gabalfa	811	10.9	137.8	4.5
Grangetown	1221	8.9	199.3	5.4
Heath	1327	11.7	35.5	2.8
Lisvane/Pontprennau★	1039	9.6	178.6	3.3
Llandaff	1329	15.2	34.4	3.3
Llandaff North	864	10.9	110.7	5.6
Llanishen	1688	11.0	85.9	4.2
Llanrumney	789	7.3	145.0	4.6
Pentwyn	1189	8.5	61.8	4.0
Pentyrch	640	18.6	30.9	4.4
Plasnewydd	1711	10.7	75.8	3.5
Rhiwbina	1375	12.6	14.7	1.6
Riverside	1556	13.5	59.9	5.0
Roath	1359	12.0	48.0	2.9
Rumney	703	8.1	133.6	4.6
Splott	1026	8.9	235.3	5.9
Trowbridge	1239	8.9	188.1	5.3
Whitchurch/Tongwynlais	1991	13.2	38.7	3.1
Cardiff	31944	10.9	76.7	4.2

★ Aggregated wards

(d) Population Change : Welsh- and Non-Welsh-speakers

The discussion so far has focused specifically on shifts in numbers and percentages of Welsh-speakers within ward areas, and no mention has yet been made of associated changes in that section of the population that is non-Welsh-speaking. It is important that these latter changes be addressed since they help to elucidate the differences in Welsh-speaking percentages discussed above. More than that, they also serve to illustrate just how varied and complex circumstances can be at the local level.

This is amply demonstrated in Table 10, the structure of which requires some explanation. In the first instance, the tabulation differentiates between those ward areas that recorded positive and negative differences in proportions of Welsh-speakers for the period 1991 and 2001. It then sub-divides these two broad categories according to whether or not absolute numbers of Welsh-speakers within them increased or decreased. The patterns associated with these measures (i.e. differences in percentages and rates and directions of change in absolute numbers) have already been analyzed. In Table 10 these data are broken down further according to the direction of change in non-Welsh-speaking populations. The resultant classification distinguishes eight categories to which ward areas can potentially belong, but two of these are logically and statistically redundant (i.e. cannot apply). The tabulation simply records the number of ward areas falling into each of the six categories of change that have been identified. The distribution of these wards is shown in Figure 10. It is unnecessary to enter into a detailed analysis of the resultant patterns, but a number of general comments on each of the categories are in order.

By far the most dominant of the categories in terms of its areal extent is that comprising wards – 180 in all – where a decline in the percentage of the population able to speak Welsh between 1991 and 2001 (i.e. differences in percentages were negative) resulted from the combined effect of a decrease in the absolute number of Welsh-speakers, and an increase in the number of non-Welsh-speakers. This category(Category 1 in Figure

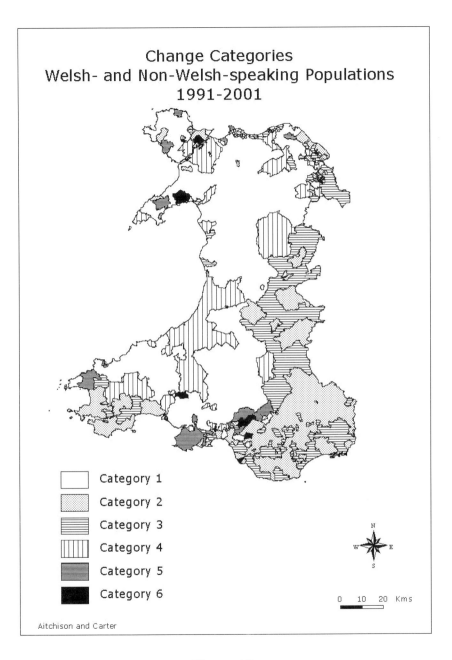

Change Categories
Welsh- and Non-Welsh-speaking Populations
1991-2001

Category 1
Category 2
Category 3
Category 4
Category 5
Category 6

0   10   20   Kms

Aitchison and Carter

Figure 10.

77

Table 10
Ward Areas

Differences in Welsh-speaking Percentages : 1991–2001
Directions of Change in Welsh-speaking and Non-Welsh-speaking
Populations*

Welsh-speaking Percentage Differences	Welsh-speaking Population Decrease		Welsh-speaking Population Increase	
	Non-Welsh Decrease	Non-Welsh Increase	Non-Welsh Decrease	Non-Welsh Increase
Negative	33 [5]	180 [1]	–	86 [4]
Positive	13 [6]	–	289 [2]	163 [3]
Totals	46	180	289	249

*Numbers in square brackets refer to categories depicted in Figure 10.

10), which embraces much of the traditional heartland and areas beyond, seemingly identifies the classic migratory situation of an outflow of Welsh-speakers and an inflow of non-Welsh-speakers. The outflow may represent a long-term departure from the area of Welsh-speakers (e.g. because of limited employment opportunities, or lack of access to affordable housing), but it is no doubt partly affected by the fact that for the 2001 census students in higher education from the areas concerned will be recorded elsewhere. Between 1991 and 2001 the total population aged 3 and over in these Category 1 wards generally increased by up to 10 per cent. However, a number of wards recorded decreases, including a cluster of areas dominating the hills and uplands of north Wales (Figure 11).

78

In terms of numbers of wards, the largest category (289) is that in which increases in the proportions of Welsh-speakers for the period 1991–2001 were based on advances in absolute numbers of Welsh-speakers and decreases in numbers of non-Welsh-speakers. The areas concerned are mainly located in south-east Wales (including the old coal-mining valleys) and south Pembrokeshire (Category 2). Many of the wards in this category recorded decreases in populations aged 3 and over for the inter-censal period (Figure 11). The growth in the number and proportion of Welsh-speakers would appear therefore to derive mainly from an expansion in the number of people from within the existing community who have learnt the language, especially in the younger age groups.

The third largest group of wards (163) involves those areas, mainly in the borderlands and in the growth regions of south Wales (Category 3) where the numbers of Welsh-speakers and non–Welsh-speakers have both expanded quite strongly (Figure 10). The significant feature here, however, is the fact that the increase in numbers of Welsh-speakers outpaced that of non-Welsh-speakers – hence the increase in the proportion of Welsh-speakers between 1991 and 2001. This advance stems from the inflow of Welsh-speakers (e.g. to the Cardiff region) and the expansion of Welsh-medium education. Another distinctive category depicted in Figure 10 (Category 4) is that comprising wards in which the proportion of Welsh-speakers decreased between 1991 and 2001, despite the fact that numbers of Welsh-speakers actually increased. The reason for this is that numbers of non-Welsh-speakers in the areas concerned also increased, and at a greater rate. The 86 wards in this category form a number of clear and quite large clusters. Of note is the extensive area dominating much of Ceredigion and north-eastern Carmarthenshire, a grouping of wards in north Pembrokeshire, areas to the east of Lake Vyrnwy centred on the settlements of Llanfair Caereinion, Llanfihangel-yng-Ngwynfa and Llanrhaeadr-ym-Mochnant in northern Powys, wards around the Vale of Clwyd, and a set of wards in the Caernarfon-Bangor region. Over the

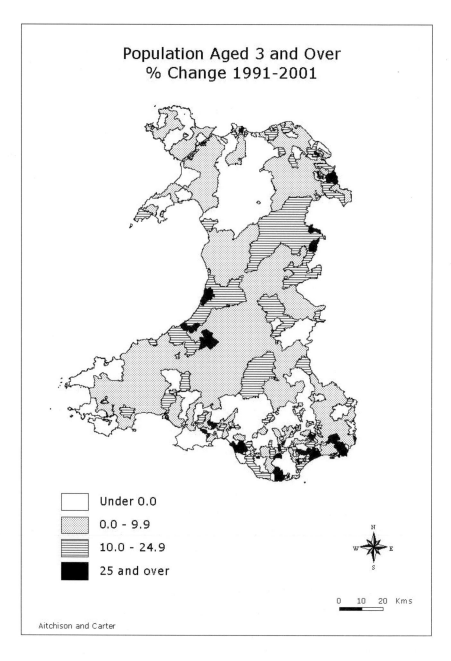

Population Aged 3 and Over
% Change 1991-2001

Under 0.0

0.0 - 9.9

10.0 - 24.9

25 and over

0   10   20   Kms

Aitchison and Carter

Figure 11.

period many of these localities experienced a fairly substantial growth in population (Figure 11). While general in-migration no doubt accounts for much of this growth, it is worth noting (yet again) that some of these areas have been affected by the enumeration of students in centres of higher education. Examples are the towns of Aberystwyth, Lampeter and Bangor. The two remaining categories involve small numbers of wards. The one (Category 5) comprises 33 wards where proportions of Welsh-speakers fell between 1991 and 2001, with numbers of Welsh-speakers and non-Welsh-speakers both recording decreases. The areas concerned are widely distributed, but a small, fragmented concentration is to be seen in south Wales, embracing the Gower Pensinsula and wards in the Vale of Neath. The final category (Category 6) involves just 13 wards. In these areas proportions of Welsh-speakers increased, despite the fact that absolute numbers of Welsh-speakers actually declined over the ten year period. This is because the number of non-Welsh-speakers declined at a greater rate. The wards in this category are again very widely dispersed.

Having drawn attention to population changes and their impact on the absolute and relative strength of the Welsh-speaking community, it is appropriate briefly to consider the crucial and highly contentious issue of migration. Unfortunately, the census is capable of shedding only limited light on this matter for it simply records changes of address in the year before the day that the census was undertaken. Furthermore, whether or not the migrants concerned are Welsh-speakers is only partially recorded. Since the censuses in England, Scotland and Northern Ireland contained no question on Welsh-language skills it is impossible to determine how many of those leaving Wales during the relevant period were actually able to speak the language. The loss-side of the language equation is therefore missing. The fact that for the 2001 census students were returned at their place of study confounds matters further, and can affect assessments greatly. The situation, as it applies in places such as Bangor, Aberystwyth and Lampeter has already been alluded to, but it applies to all towns with centres of higher education. Aberystwyth, for example, recorded 478 in-migrants from outside the United Kingdom, the great majority of whom must have been overseas students taking up residence. Interestingly, University records for Aberystwyth indicate that the total number of students from outside the UK in residence in session 2002–3 was 573. The limitations of the data are therefore only too apparent, and must be taken into account in any interpretation of migratory trends.

Discussion of these problems and deficiencies is all rather academic since, at the time of writing, the Office for National Statistics had not released data on migration with details of the language of in-migrants. The only tabulations published refer to numbers moving in and out of local authority areas. In regard to these it is worth noting that all counties in Wales, except three, recorded net gains. The three with net losses were Blaenau Gwent, Merthyr Tydfil and Torfaen. The greatest net gain was, as might be expected, at Cardiff with a total inward movement of 16,573 balanced by an outward loss of 12,994, giving a net gain of 3,579. Precisely how many of these were Welsh-speakers from other parts of Wales it is not possible to say, but it has been flows of this nature that have contributed so significantly to the growth in numbers of Welsh-speakers in the capital. It is also noteworthy that the next highest gain was recorded by Ceredigion, although how much this was due to student numbers it is again impossible to tell. Whatever the truth of the matter, the county's inward gain of 5,380 was offset by an outward movement of 4,040. Similar patterns occur in the other rural counties. Of course, this is only fragmentary evidence on which too much stress should not be placed. Such as it is, however, it confirms the continuation of trends which were active in the last quarter of the last century, continued rural depopulation masked by a dominant re-population. Referring back to the data for 1991 it is possible to infer that these movements have been contributory to the decline of Welsh speech in the once so solid heartland regions.

(iii) Urban and Rural Contexts

In analyzing variations in the number and percentage dominance of Welsh-speakers reference has frequently been made to differences between rural and urban areas. It is appropriate at this point in the discussion to consider these differences more fully and directly. To this end the 881 wards have been sub-divided into two categories according to the density of the population aged 3 years and over. The threshold adopted is a density of 200 persons per square kilometre. This threshold has been determined empirically with a view to distinguishing not only the main urban-industrial regions of south and north-east Wales, but also the smaller rural market towns scattered throughout other parts of Wales. While it cannot be regarded as a highly sophisticated measure of levels of either urbanization or 'rurality', for purposes of discussion the density threshold does serve to differentiate between the two broad domains. Based on this criterion 561 wards are classed as 'urban'. They have an average population density of 1,511 km^2, with a maximum figure of 9,785 km^2. As for the more 'rural' wards – 320 in number – the average population density is 65 km^2. Here values range from 4 to 198.

In 2001 some 61.5 per cent (354,170) of all Welsh-speakers in Wales were resident in urban wards (c.f. 78.4 per cent of the total population aged 3 and over). In aggregate 'urban' Welsh-speakers accounted for 16 per cent of the 'urban' population aged three and over. The equivalent percentage for 'rural' areas is 37. Table 11 shows that the situation varies greatly at the local authority level. In Cardiff and Blaenau Gwent all of the wards (and therefore all of the Welsh-speakers) are classed as 'urban'. As is to be expected, in the other local authorities with significant urban populations the proportion of Welsh-speakers who are classed as 'urban' is very high, often exceeding 90 per cent. While equivalent percentages are generally much lower in the mainly rural areas, it is significant that even here the proportions of 'urban' Welsh can also be quite high. In Gwynedd and Ynys Môn, for example, just over 40 per cent of Welsh-speakers were enumerated in 'urban' wards. Here the main concentrations

Table 11
Welsh-speakers : Urban and Rural Wards

Local Authority Area	% Welsh-speakers in Urban Wards	Welsh-speakers as % of Population in Urban Wards	Welsh-speakers as % of Population in Rural Wards
Blaenau Gwent	100.0	9.1	0.0
Bridgend	87.4	10.5	11.1
Caerphilly	95.5	10.9	11.2
Carmarthenshire	40.9	42.0	57.7
Cardiff	100.0	10.9	0.0
Ceredigion	32.3	44.4	56.3
Conwy	69.5	24.3	53.6
Denbighshire	56.9	21.2	37.7
Flintshire	74.4	13.0	18.7
Gwynedd	42.6	70.4	67.5
Merthyr Tydfil	93.4	10.0	10.8
Monmouthshire	62.3	9.3	8.6
Neath	64.1	15.7	23.3
Newport	92.4	9.6	8.8
Pembrokeshire	37.5	16.0	27.1
Powys	26.5	19.1	21.6
Rhondda Cynon Taf	98.9	12.2	17.7
Swansea	94.8	13.0	18.6
Torfaen	98.6	10.7	10.6
Vale of Glamorgan	79.8	10.9	11.9
Wrexham	85.7	15.0	11.9
Ynys Môn	44.2	57.6	61.8
Wales	**61.5**	**16.1**	**36.6**

84

are associated with areas in and around the towns of Caernarfon, Llangefni, Pwllheli, Porthmadog and Bala.

For each of the local authorities Table 11 also records the proportions of the respective urban and rural populations aged three and over who are able to speak Welsh. The data are revealing. They show for instance that, whilst the proportions of Welsh-speakers in urban areas are generally lower than in their more rural counterparts, there are some marked regional differences. Thus, in Gwynedd percentages of Welsh-speakers are higher in urban wards than they are in rural wards (70.4 per cent as opposed to 67.5 per cent). Urban percentages are also relatively high in Ynys Môn (57.6 per cent), Ceredigion (44.4 per cent) and Carmarthenshire (42.0 per cent). The sharpest disparities between urban and rural areas are recorded for Conwy and Denbighshire. Here, although large numbers of Welsh-speakers live in urban wards, the proportions of Welsh-speakers are actually quite low. The localities concerned are mainly located along the coast of north Wales, and, as favoured retirement areas, have experienced considerable in-migration, dominantly from outside of Wales. This has inevitably diluted the relative strength of the Welsh-speaking population. In the rural hinterland the proportion of Welsh-speakers is of a much higher order. For most of the other local authority areas in Wales the percentage of Welsh-speakers within urban wards generally ranges between 10 and 15. For rural wards the equivalent percentages are seen to be generally higher, but more variable.

Overall, these statistics serve to affirm the fact that much of the Welsh spoken in Wales takes place in an urban context. While rural areas may dominate the Welsh-speaking map (mainly because of their size), it could be argued that, in purely quantitative terms, it is in the more densely-settled centres of population that the future strength of the language lies. As Aitchison and Carter have observed (Aitchison and Carter, 2000), this poses problems for a minority language as it seeks to survive in transactional environments where English is the dominant medium of communication and where more cosmopolitan forces are at work.

(iv) Age Profiles

Previous studies of language change in Wales have emphasized the critical role played by education in the promotion of Welsh, especially in the pre-school, primary and secondary spheres. Over recent decades these spheres have stimulated a major rejuvenation of the language throughout Wales, but have had a particularly dramatic impact in certain areas. This is clearly demonstrated in Table 12 where proportions of the Welsh-speaking population within each of five age bands are recorded for the 22 local authorities and for Wales as a whole. It shows that in the main growth areas of the language by far the greatest percentage of Welsh-speakers are under 16 years of age. Thus, they account for more than half of speakers in Blaenau Gwent, Caerphilly, Monmouthshire, Newport and Torfaen. In the rural heartland these percentages are noticeably lower, generally less than 25 per cent. Proportions of Welsh-speakers between 16 and 44 years of age are fairly tightly clustered between 25 per cent and 35 per cent, but a distinctively high value is seen to be recorded by Cardiff – 41.6 per cent. This figure no doubt reflects the steady migration into the area of young Welsh-speaking professionals, and the presence of Welsh-speaking students from other parts of Wales. The final two age groups account for fewer Welsh-speakers, but the relatively high values returned by the older industrial regions of Carmarthenshire, Swansea and Neath/Port Talbot are worth highlighting since they again point to the frailty of the language in these particular areas.

Figure 12 charts proportions of Welsh-speakers aged between 3 and 15 years. It confirms the sharp divide between the heartland areas of the north and west, where percentages are generally less than 25, and the remaining regions where they are often in excess of 40. The highest percentages of all (over 60 per cent) apply in much of eastern and southern Monmouthshire, the Newport region and the eastern valleys of the old South Wales coalfield. A comparison of this distribution pattern with that for 1991 (see Aitchison and Carter, 2000, 107) is particularly revealing for

Table 12

Welsh-speaking Population by Age Groups

Local Authority Area	% 3 – 15 Years	% 16 – 44 Years	% 45 – 64 Years	% 65 Years and over
Blaenau Gwent	68.2	22.0	6.1	3.7
Bridgend	40.3	32.3	13.2	14.1
Caerphilly	54.5	32.4	8.1	5.0
Cardiff	39.9	41.6	11.6	6.9
Carmarthenshire	19.6	31.1	25.6	23.7
Ceredigion	21.6	34.4	24.2	19.8
Conwy	24.5	33.1	21.8	20.6
Denbighshire	25.3	32.6	21.9	20.1
Flintshire	41.1	33.1	14.7	11.1
Gwynedd	21.1	37.6	23.2	18.1
Merthyr Tydfil	44.6	31.4	11.3	12.7
Monmouthshire	66.4	17.2	10.0	6.4
Neath/Port Talbot	28.1	27.8	21.1	23.0
Newport	70.2	18.9	6.5	4.3
Pembrokeshire	33.5	27.8	21.3	17.4
Powys	32.2	28.6	20.0	19.2
Rhondda Cynon Taf	41.9	35.5	10.9	11.7
Swansea	27.6	26.1	21.3	25.0
Torfaen	69.5	21.2	5.7	3.6
Vale of Glamorgan	47.9	30.1	13.3	8.7
Wrexham	33.0	29.6	18.8	18.6
Ynys Môn	20.8	36.6	24.9	17.6
Wales	31.2	32.3	19.5	17.0

★ Based on CAS tabulations

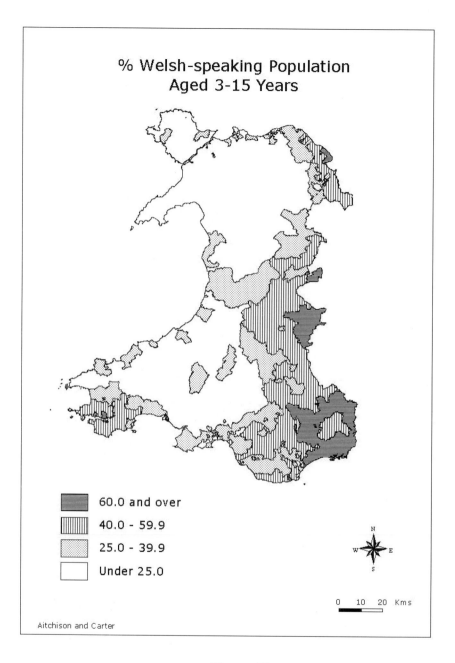

% Welsh-speaking Population
Aged 3-15 Years

60.0 and over
40.0 - 59.9
25.0 - 39.9
Under 25.0

Aitchison and Carter

Figure 12.

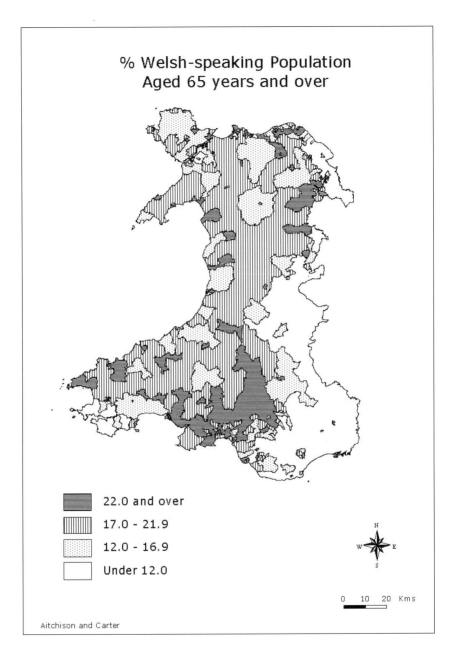

Figure 13.

it shows just how strong the rejuvenation of the language has been in 'Outer Wales'. This is most particularly the case as far as the situation in Monmouthshire and Newport is concerned. Figures for the heartland have not changed to any marked degree. Here age profiles for the Welsh-speaking community remain much more balanced, with no heavy skew towards the younger age group. The only exception to this is a strengthening of the age group in wards across mid –Wales and south Gwynedd.

Figure 13 shows the proportion of Welsh-speakers aged 65 years and over. The distribution is very much the inverse of that displayed in Figure 12, but with some distinctive local nuances. Of particular note are the high values – in excess of 22 per cent – returned by a band of wards within what was once the western coalfield region. Included in this zone are wards within the Llanelli-Swansea areas and the vales of Tawe and Neath. This band stretches on into south-central Wales, and even links up with the Tregaron ward on the eastern edge of Ceredigion. The proportion of Welsh-speakers aged 65 and over is also seen to be high in the Glyn-Ceiriog, Chirk and Wrexham area, and along the coastal margins of north Wales. Although equally strong values are recorded by a dispersed collection of wards within the traditional heartland, in this area proportions are very similar, ranging generally between 17 per cent and 22 per cent. That said, it is evident that quite large numbers of wards in the heartland, especially along the coast of west Wales, have age profiles in which those aged 65 years and over figure even less prominently. All in all the situation is very variable, with sharp local discontinuities characterizing the age structures of the Welsh-speaking population.

(v) Social and Economic Contexts

In the introductory discussion reference was made to the importance of the new employment opportunities that have opened up for Welsh-speakers, and the importance of this both in helping to limit out-migration from Wales and in consolidating the language base. As has been noted, the de-industrialization of Wales has been accompanied by a marked switch from jobs in manufacturing to professional and administrative posts where those who can offer a facility in Welsh have some advantage. Thus, the ability to speak Welsh has become associated with higher status positions. This is well-illustrated in various census tabulations.

Table 13 is interesting for it draws attention to significant differences in terms of major occupational groups. For example, if the two top groups (Managers and Senior Officials, Professional Occupations) are taken together Welsh-speakers are seen to be more strongly represented than the population at large, and especially that section of the population with no knowledge of Welsh whatsoever. However, it is clear that this is derived from a preponderance in the category of 'Professional Occupations', for Welsh-speakers are under-represented (relatively) in the category 'Managers and Senior Officials'. Within this latter group there is a further disparity. In the breakdown into 'Corporate Managers' and 'Managers and Proprietors in Agriculture and Services' the ratio for all employed is 69:31, for those with no knowledge of Welsh 70:30, but for Welsh-speakers it is 65:35. This draws attention to a somewhat weaker representation of Welsh-speakers in the commanding heights of the economy. However, the crucial aspect is where power lies in the sense of the future influence on language issues, and it is much more likely to rest with the professional classes rather than with business managers. Table 14 indicates that as far as those employed in professional occupations are concerned, the Welsh-speaking representation is overwhelmingly focused on teaching and research, and to such an extent that the proportions in all the other categories are lower than those for the population at large. There is, however, a marked under-representation of Welsh-speakers in science and technology occupations.

Three further points are worth making. Firstly, although the differences in the 'Associate Professional and Technical' category are of a minor order, there are contrasts when it is broken down into the component groups (Table 15). Here again the under-representation of Welsh-speakers in

91

science and technology and in business is apparent. So, too, is the over-representation in culture and media occupations. The second point concerns the greater proportion of Welsh-speakers in skilled trades. This may be unexpected, but again reference to the categories making up this group shows that the difference results from the predominance of Welsh-speakers in skilled agricultural trades where some 33.4 per cent are found, as against 16.1 per cent for all employed and only 11.4 per cent for those with no language skills. Finally, at the lower end of the occupational scale, in what are termed 'Elementary Occupations', the representation of Welsh-speakers is lower than that for the employed population as a whole (Table 13).

Together, these various data confirm the movement of Welsh-speakers into professional occupations, especially in education, and into posts associated with culture and the media. There is a clear under-representation in commerce and business, and in science and technology. This occupational profile conforms to that of a population directed towards public service and the media, rather than to more entrepreneurial activities. Given this conclusion it is perhaps surprising that there is a smaller proportion employed in 'Administration and Secretarial Occupations' and that the breakdown into administrative and secretarial categories shows no difference between the population at large and the active Welsh-speaking population. Even so, together, the employment statistics indicate that in the process of economic re-structuring that characterised the last quarter of the 20th century, Welsh-speakers have managed to command higher level occupations. As has already been argued, this development is linked to, and partly responsible for, the rise in status of the language and the reversal of the decline of earlier times. It is also significant in terms of the explicit control of those levers which mould public opinion.

The broad conclusions derived from the above analysis of occupational categories are accorded further confirmation if reference is made to the National Statistics – Socio-Economic Classification (NS-SeC). These are displayed in Table 16. Here the 'Large Employers and Higher Managerial'

Table 13

Major Occupational Groups

Occupational Groups	% All Employed	% No skills in Welsh	% Welsh- speakers
Managers and Senior Officials	12.3	12.8	9.7
Professional Occupations	10.5	9.4	14.4
Associate Prof. and Tech. Occupations	13.0	12.7	12.6
Admin. and Secretarial Occupations	12.3	12.1	11.9
Skilled Trades	13.6	13.1	15.5
Personal Services	7.5	7.1	8.5
Sales and Customer Services	6.9	8.2	7.3
Process, Plant and Machine Operators	10.3	10.8	8.1
Elementary Occupations	13.5	13.8	12.0

Table 14

Professional Occupations

Sub-Category	% All Employed	% No skills in Welsh	% Welsh-speakers
Science and Technology	24.9	29.2	14.4
Health Professionals	9.1	10.2	6.6
Teaching and Research	46.3	39.8	62.4
Business and Public Services	19.7	20.8	16.6

Table 15

Associate Professional and Technical Occupations

Sub-Groups	% All Employed	% No skills in Welsh	% Welsh-speakers
Science and Technology	16.4	17.5	13.2
Health and Social Welfare	31.6	30.2	34.7
Protective Services	9.5	9.6	9.5
Culture, Media and Sports	11.0	10.0	15.5
Business and Public Services	31.5	32.7	27.1

Table 16

National Statistics : Socio-Economic Classification

Socio-economic Group	% All People	% No knowledge of Welsh	% Welsh-speakers
Large employers and higher managerial	2.2	2.3	1.6
Higher professional	3.7	3.6	3.8
Lower managerial and professional	16.1	15.3	18.2
Intermediate	8.0	8.0	7.8
Small employers and own account workers	7.1	6.7	8.8
Lower supervisory and technical	7.8	8.0	6.7
Semi-routine	12.2	12.7	10.6
Routine	9.9	10.6	8.0
Never worked or long term unemployed	3.8	4.2	2.6
Not classified	29.1	28.5	31.8

Table 17

Highest Level of Qualifications by Age

Age	Qualification Level	% All People	% No Knowledge of Welsh	% Welsh-speakers
16-24	None	17.9	18.3	18.4
	Level 4/5	9.5	9.0	10.7
25-34	None	16.2	18.1	9.5
	Level 4/5	23.6	21.8	31.1
35-44	None	24.0	26.2	16.2
	Level 4/5	20.6	18.7	28.2
45-54	None	34.9	37.2	28.1
	Level 4/5	19.7	17.5	28.2
55-59	None	46.2	48.5	40.7
	Level 4/5	15.6	13.6	22.8

Note. None means no qualification. Level 4/5 means the possession of a first or higher degree, HNC or HND. It also includes qualified doctors, dentists, nurses, midwives and health visitors.

occupations show a greater proportion of non-Welsh-speakers, but for the 'Higher Professional' and 'Lower Managerial and Professional' categories it is to the Welsh-speakers that this applies. Table 16 again emphasises the greater preponderance of non-Welsh-speakers in the lower socio-economic categories. The large proportion of Welsh-speakers in the 'Not classified' group warrants comment, for it derives in the main from the inclusion within the category of full-time students. While full-time students in the 'Not Classified' category accounted for 7.2 per cent of the total active population and 6.3 per cent of those with no knowledge of Welsh, the figure for Welsh-speakers was 11.3 per cent. This commitment to higher education within the Welsh-speaking population is further underlined in Table 17 which records the highest levels of qualifications by age group and by ability to speak Welsh.

Apart from the somewhat anomalous 16–24 age group, across all categories there are smaller proportions of Welsh-speakers with no qualifications, and higher proportions with Level 4/5 qualifications. It is this manifest variation in levels of educational and professional training and achievement, that underpins the differences which appear in the occupation and socio-economic classifications previously discussed. In certain areas the increase in numbers of Welsh-speakers has been closely associated with the growth of the professional classes, and the differences between Welsh-speakers and those with no knowledge of Welsh are particularly evident in the age groups between 25 and 54. Most of these people were in their twenties and thirties in the 1970s and 80s, and they represent the power house of the movement for the advance of the language. They were in many cases the sons and daughters of working-class parents who, traditionally in Wales, were committed to education both for itself and as a means of escape from the limitations of jobs in mining and heavy industry and on the farm. Moving into posts in teaching, administration and the media they became the active leaders of support for the language, capable of setting the agenda over language issues and driving their concerns forward.

Having examined at some length the key language indicator – ability to speak Welsh – the discussion now moves on to consider the issue of literacy within the Welsh-speaking population.

5. LITERACY PROFILES : SPEAKING, READING AND WRITING

A s in previous enumerations, the 2001 census distinguishes three categories of Welsh-speakers – those who are only 'able to speak, but not read or write', those who are 'able to speak and read, but not write', and those who are 'able to speak, read and write'. Having looked at these categories together in the analysis of numbers of speakers, it is worthwhile considering each of them separately, for as measures of levels of literacy they help to shed further light on regional variations in the general resilience and quality of the language. Once again the relevant statistical data can be processed in different ways. It is meaningful, for instance, to measure the relative strength of the various categories by determining percentages in relation to the total population aged three and over, the population that claims a knowledge of Welsh and the population able to speak Welsh. Each of these sets of percentages is presented in Tables 2, 3 and 18 for Wales as a whole and for local authorities.

At the 2001 census the number of people able to speak, but not read or write Welsh totalled 79,310 (Table 1). This represented 2.8 per cent of the population aged three and over (Table 2), 9.9 per cent of all those who professed some knowledge of Welsh (Table 3), and 13.8 per cent of all those able to speak the language (Table 18). Whilst it is to be expected that many of those in this category will be in the very young age groups, it is evident that it will also include learners of the language and those who, for whatever reason, have not extended their knowledge of Welsh to the levels of reading and writing. An analysis of age profiles for this language category confirms that this diversity of composition applies. A third are under 16 years of age, but a further 20 per cent are 65 and over.

In terms of the total population aged 3 and over, the percentage able to speak, but not read or write Welsh, is seen to be at its highest – in excess of 4 per cent – in the main Welsh-speaking areas. Most notable in this regard are the values recorded for Carmarthenshire (7.2 per cent) and Ynys Môn (6.4 per cent). It will be recalled that these two areas also returned the highest percentages for those able to understand spoken Welsh only (Table 2). It would appear that within these particular local authorities significant numbers of people have a fairly basic appreciation of the language, and that literacy levels are lower than might well have been expected. This does not apply to anything like the same extent in the other main Welsh-speaking areas. Here, it would appear that where relatively high percentages pertain they are more likely to reflect the presence of a substantial body of young speakers who will eventually move on to read and write the language. Throughout the remaining regions of Wales percentages are frequently less than 3 per cent, and especially so in the most densely populated areas of the south.

If the number of those able to speak, but not read or write Welsh, is related to the total number with a knowledge of the language then a slightly different regional picture emerges. Table 3 shows, for instance, that at the local authority level the highest percentages are recorded by counties in south-east Wales – Blaenau Gwent (14.3 per cent), Torfaen (13.3 per cent), Newport (13.3 per cent) and Monmouthshire (12.5 per cent). It will be recalled that it was in these areas that numbers of Welsh-speakers grew most rapidly between 1991 and 2001 (see Table 5). The higher than average percentages might therefore reflect the early stages of language acquisition in the regions concerned. Interestingly, the lowest values of all are returned by local authorities in two very differing regions – Gwynedd (7.6 per cent) and Ceredigion (8.1 per cent) within the rural heartland, and Rhondda Cynon Taf (7.9 per cent) and Bridgend (8.1 per cent) in industrial/urban south Wales.

Finally, Table 18 expresses the number of Welsh-speakers who are unable to read or write the language as a percentage of the total Welsh-speaking population. The highest values are again recorded by the main urban authorities across south Wales. Blaenau Gwent stands out with a particularly high percentage (21.0), but also of note are those recorded by Swansea (18.7 per cent), Newport (18.5 per cent) and Neath/Port Talbot (18.3 per cent). The percentage returned for Cardiff (12.9 per cent) is much lower than in these urban centres, reflecting no doubt the sizeable flow into the area of more literate Welsh-speakers. Many of these will have come from the Welsh-speaking heartland where the proportion of speakers unable to read and write Welsh is also very low. The lowest percentages of all – less than 10 – apply in Gwynedd (8.4 per cent) and Ceredigion (9.6 per cent). In these areas, as has already been noted, literacy levels are generally of a much higher order. Figure 14 classifies wards into four groups based on quartile values. The resulting pattern re–affirms the broad distinction between the Welsh-speaking heartland and the more Anglicized areas of south Wales and the borderland. In these latter regions percentages are at their highest (over 18.5) in central and south-eastern parts of Pembrokeshire, and in the area between Llanelli and the Aman Valley. Further to the east similarly high figures are recorded by wards in the local authorities of Caerphilly, Bleanau Gwent, parts of Newport, and eastern Monmouthshire. Along the rest of the borderland the pattern is very fragmented, but high values are returned by small clusters in central Brecknock, the eastern fringes of Montgomeryshire and the northern coastal sections of Flintshire. Within the heartland itself percentages are generally below 10. It is worth noting, however, that this region does include a number of areas, mainly in the more Anglicized localities where percentages are well above average. Examples, are Trefriew in the Conwy Valley, wards around Aberystwyth and between Newport and Cardigan in Pembrokeshire. It will be recalled that these, and neighbouring areas, also scored highly in terms of percentages only able to understand the

Table 18

Census Language Categories

As a Percentage of Population Able to Speak Welsh : 2001

Local Authority Area	Speaks Welsh, but does not read or write Welsh	Speaks and reads Welsh, but does not write Welsh	Speaks, Reads and Writes Welsh
	%	%	%
Blaenau Gwent	21.0	6.6	72.4
Bridgend	15.2	8.3	76.5
Caerphilly	15.8	6.1	78.1
Cardiff	12.9	6.5	80.6
Carmarthenshire	14.4	7.8	77.8
Ceredigion	9.6	5.3	85.1
Conwy	13.8	6.7	79.6
Denbighshire	14.0	6.7	79.3
Flintshire	15.1	7.5	77.4
Gwynedd	8.4	3.4	88.3
Merthyr Tydfil	17.1	9.7	73.3
Monmouthshire	17.8	6.6	75.7
Neath/Port Talbot	18.3	9.5	72.1
Newport	18.5	6.4	75.1
Pembrokeshire	16.3	7.6	76.0
Powys	15.3	8.0	76.6
Rhondda Cynon Taf	13.5	6.8	79.7
Swansea	18.7	10.3	71.0
Torfaen	18.0	6.5	75.5
Vale of Glamorgan	14.5	6.2	79.6
Wrexham	16.3	8.1	75.5
Ynys Môn	10.7	4.9	84.4
Wales	**13.8**	**6.7**	**79.6**

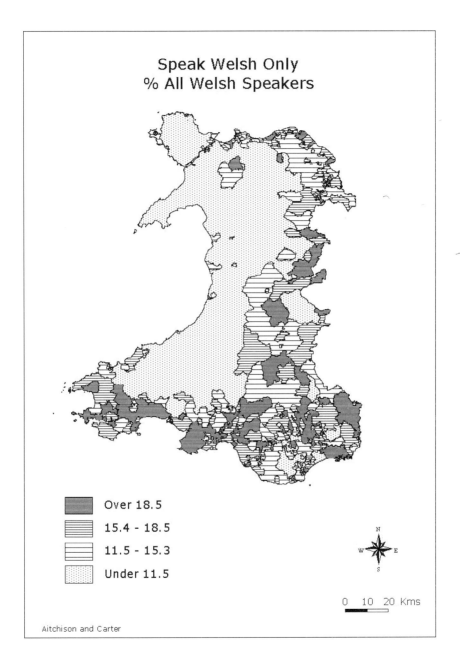

Speak Welsh Only
% All Welsh Speakers

Over 18.5

15.4 - 18.5

11.5 - 15.3

Under 11.5

0   10   20 Kms

Aitchison and Carter

Figure 14.

101

language (see Figures 3 and 4). The factors underpinning the two sets of distributions are likely to be fairly similar. Together, they confirm the relatively low standing of the language within the areas concerned.

The literacy category identifying those who can speak and read Welsh, but who are unable to write in the language, is small numerically, accounting for just 1.4 per cent of the population aged 3 and over, 4.8 per cent of those claiming some knowledge of Welsh, and 6.7 per cent of all Welsh-speakers. In terms of the latter, it is evident from Table 18 that, while values for local authorities are quite concentrated around the average, three urban regions in South Wales return particularly high figures – Swansea (10.3 per cent), Merthyr Tydfil (9.7 per cent) and Neath/Port Talbot (9.5 per cent). At ward level the percentage of the Welsh-speaking population that is able to read, but not write Welsh, varies between 0.0 per cent (Castle, Monmouthshire) and 18.8 per cent (Coity, Brigend). The mean value is 7.1 per cent. The distribution displayed in Figure 15 broadly repeats the pattern outlined above for those only able to speak Welsh. But in this case it is apparent that relatively high percentages are also recorded in more western parts of Pembrokeshire, and for much of the former district of Brecknock, especially the region lying between Brecon and Builth Wells.

Table 2 indicates that only 16.3 per cent of the population aged 3 and over are fully literate, being able to speak, read and write Welsh. This may seem low, particularly when compared with the proportion claiming an ability to speak Welsh (20.5 per cent). The difference can be partially explained by the presence of young speakers who have not yet progressed to the stage of being able to read and write the language. Whilst this is the case, it is evident from the discussion thus far that in certain regions levels of literacy are of a very low magnitude, and that many in the older age groups have only a basic ability to converse in the language, possibly a reflection of the educational system of their youth when English was the exclusive medium of instruction. Expressed in relation to the population who claim to have a knowledge of Welsh, the proportion able to speak, read and write the language is 57.4 per cent (Table 3); as a proportion of those able to speak Welsh it increases to a substantial 79.6 per cent (Table 18). A comparison with the census returns for 1991 would suggest a major increase in the standard of literacy of Welsh-speakers. At that time the recorded number of speakers able to read and write Welsh stood at 369,609 (c.f. 457,946 in 2001), with an associated percentage figure of 72.6 per cent. Absolute numbers, therefore, increased by a massive 24 per cent. At the local authority level percentages are seen to be quite tightly clustered around the average, with values ranging from 72.4 per cent in Blaenau Gwent to 88.3 per cent in Gwynedd, with the overall average standing at 77.7 per cent (Table 18). The marked increase in the level of literacy among the Welsh-speaking community is forcefully demonstrated at ward level if the distribution displayed in Figure 16 is compared with a similarly structured map for 1991 (Aitchison and Carter, 2000, 101). From this it is evident that wards where the proportions of speakers with an ability to both read and write the language exceed 85 per cent now cover a much more extensive area. In 1991 such areas comprised a broken series of cores, now these are seen to have coalesced, forming a solid swathe across the traditional heartland of the north and west. Forty wards have percentages in excess of 90 per cent – four in Conwy, six in Ynys Môn and 30 in Gwynedd. The highest figure recorded is 95.6 per cent for Llanuwchllyn in Gwynedd. Furthermore, in mapping 1991 data it was appropriate to recognize wards with values of below 45 per cent, and between 45 per cent and 55 per cent. Now only one ward has a value of less than 55 per cent – 51.9 per cent for Overmonnow, Monmouthshire. As to wards where less than 75 per cent of speakers are able to read and write Welsh, these define an arcuate band stretching from central Pembrokeshire in the west, through the old industrial parts of south-east Carmarthenshire, Swansea, Neath and the Aman valley, and on into central regions of the former districts of Brecknock and Radnor. Beyond this

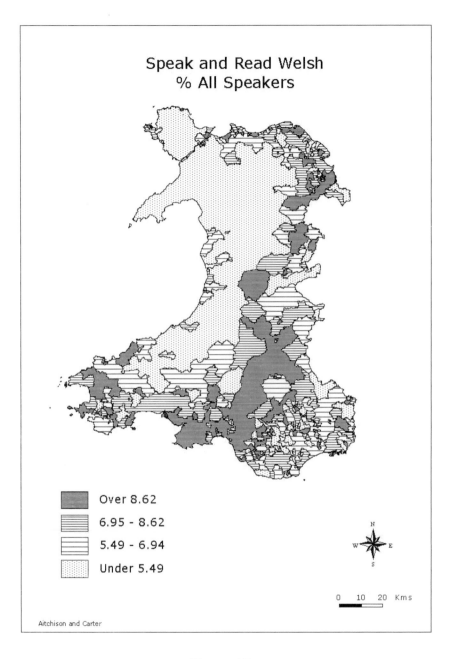

Speak and Read Welsh
% All Speakers

Over 8.62
6.95 - 8.62
5.49 - 6.94
Under 5.49

0   10   20   Kms

Aitchison and Carter

Figure 15.

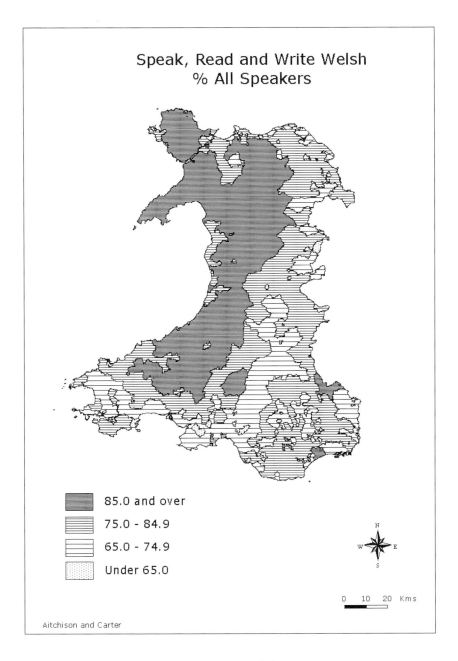

Speak, Read and Write Welsh
% All Speakers

85.0 and over

75.0 - 84.9

65.0 - 74.9

Under 65.0

0   10   20   Kms

Aitchison and Carter

Figure 16.

105

zone, in the borderland, similar percentages are recorded by a fairly large but scattered number of wards. In the traditional heartland itself several localities have much lower values than those that prevail locally – these include wards in and around Holyhead, Beaumaris, and the outskirts of Bangor. Once again the line of linguistic erosion that cleaves the heartland in the Snowdonia region is in evidence.

Finally, it is necessary to make brief reference to the residual literacy category that is described in the 2001 census tabulations as 'other combinations of skills'. As has been noted, this category includes some speakers, but in the main it identifies those who, on the census form, indicated an ability to read but not speak or write Welsh, and those who claimed to be able to read and write, but not speak Welsh. In terms of the numbers concerned (83,661) this is quite a large category; larger even than that relating to the number able to speak, but not read or write Welsh. Figure 17 expresses the number of those with 'other combinations of skills' as a percentage of all those with some knowledge of Welsh (as defined above). The distribution highlights the significance of this category in the old industrial regions of Rhondda Cynon Taf, Neath/Port Talbot, Swansea, Bridgend and the area around Llanelli. Here a large number of wards record percentages in excess of 4.

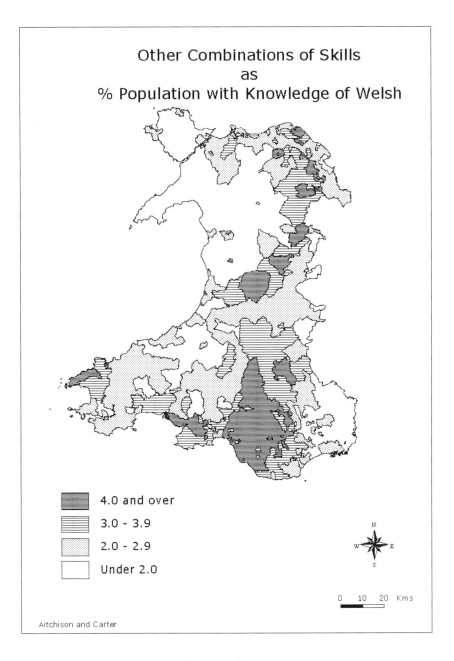

Other Combinations of Skills
as
% Population with Knowledge of Welsh

4.0 and over
3.0 - 3.9
2.0 - 2.9
Under 2.0

Aitchison and Carter

0   10   20   Kms

Figure 17.

107

6. Language Regions

The analysis thus far has examined each of the main language categories separately. From the discussions and the various maps it is evident that many of the distributions complement each other, albeit to differing degrees. Given this it seems appropriate, by way of summary, to consider whether or not coherent regional patterns emerge if the same language measures are used to derive an integrated linguistic classification of the set of 881 wards. To this end, six language variables were used in a hierarchical cluster analysis. The variables included in the analysis are:

(i)   percentage of the population aged 3 and over able to understand spoken Welsh only

(ii)   percentage of the population aged 3 and over able to speak, but not read or write Welsh

(iii)   percentage of the population aged 3 and over able to speak and read, but not write, Welsh

(iv)   percentage of the population aged 3 and over able to speak, read and write Welsh

(v)   percentage of the population aged 3 and over with other combinations of skills

(vi)   percentage of the population aged 3 and over with no knowledge of Welsh

The cluster analysis – a statistical procedure that has been widely used in the social sciences – groups the wards according how similar they are on each and everyone of the chosen variables. Using this approach it is possible to identify different levels of groupings, depending upon the degree of detail or generality deemed meaningful. Here, the aim is to proceed from the most general classification (i.e. dividing the wards into just two groups – the two cluster stage) through to the identification of six groups – the six cluster stage. The clusters recognized at the stages in between – 3, 4 and 5 – are also examined. Overall, the patterns that emerge yield a revealing and very neatly structured typology of wards. Average ward percentages for the six diagnostic variables for each of the five cluster stages are presented in Tables 19 – 23. They can be used to describe the essential attributes of the clusters that have been derived, using this particular method of analysis. The location of the wards included within the various clusters are shown in Figures 18–22.

(i) Two Cluster Stage

The division of the 881 wards into two groups results in a clear differentiation of the traditional Welsh-speaking heartland (Cluster 2), once referred to as 'Inner' Wales, from a surrounding area – 'Outer' Wales – where, over the centuries, the language has experienced successive phases of decline and retreat (Cluster 1). The 607 wards that fall within cluster 1 define an extensive zone, encompassing south Pembrokeshire, the Gower Pensinsula, the Vale of Glamorgan, the former coal-mining regions of south Wales, Monmouthshire, the former districts of Brecknock and Radnor, eastern parts of Montgomeryshire, Flintshire, the eastern fringes of Denbighshire, and a narrow strip extending along the coast of north Wales from the Point of Ayr to the Great Orme. This cluster constitutes a remarkably contiguous region (Figure 18). However, a group of four wards located within and on the edges of Aberystwyth in Ceredigion (Gogledd, Canol, Bronglais and Llanbadarn Fawr) also belong to cluster 1, and constitute a highly distinctive outlier. The special nature of development in this particular locality, with the expansion of the University and other institutions, has contributed to a dilution of the language in the area, but the fact that students were also included in the census enumeration is in part responsible for this seemingly anomalous situation. But it also

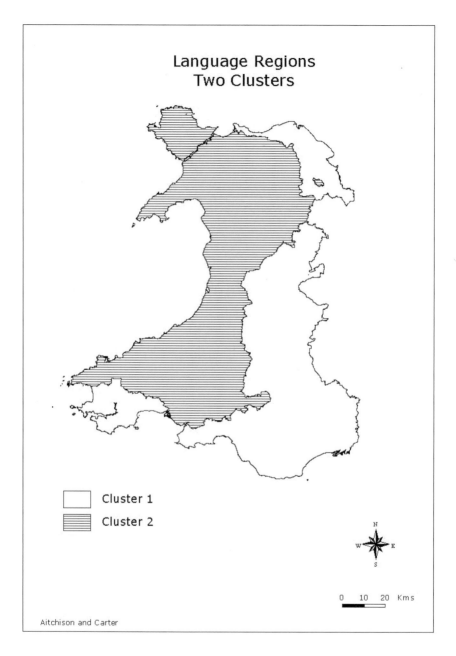

Figure 18.

suggests another element in the process of Anglicization in Welsh Wales, that of suburbanisation. In many areas suburban expansion is known to have been a factor in the spread of English speech. Although the comparisons are not strictly proper the parish of Llanbadarn Fawr, as it then was, returned 54.9 per cent Welsh-speakers in 1961. In 2001 the two wards of Llanbadarn (Padarn and Sulien) had only 30.6 per cent.

Although cluster 1 has been depicted as delimiting an essentially Anglicized region it is noteworthy that nearly half of all Welsh-speakers (47.8 per cent) are to be found within its bounds. However, it is evident that the distinguishing feature of the grouping is the high proportion of the resident populations who have no knowledge of Welsh whatsoever – 79.7 per cent (Table 19). Percentages for all of the other language variables are very low, with the proportion of the population able to speak Welsh amounting to 20.1 per cent.

The 274 wards within cluster 2 have a Welsh-speaking population of 300,365 – 52.2 per cent of the total. Together, they define another compact region dominating western and northern parts of Wales (Figure 18). Here again, however, there is a small outlying cluster comprising the wards of Dyffrin Ceiriog, Ponciau and Pant to the south-west of Wrexham. The wards that form this latter grouping delimit a contiguous area where the Welsh language has managed to maintain a relatively strong hold despite the high level of Anglicization that applies in surrounding regions. For the wards in cluster 2 the percentage of the population aged three and over who are able to speak Welsh is 57.1 per cent. Full literacy levels are also high, with 47.9 per cent the population able to speak, read and write Welsh. Interestingly, the percentage for those only able to 'understand' the language is also relatively high (8.2 per cent).

Table 19

Language regions – 2 cluster stage

	Cluster 1	Cluster 2
Number of Wards	607	274
% Understand	4.3	8.2
% Speak only	2.1	6.2
% Speak/Read	1.0	3.0
% Speak/Read/Write	9.8	47.9
% Other Skills	3.1	2.3
% No Knowledge	79.7	32.4
Number of Welsh-speakers	75274	300365

(ii) Three Cluster Stage

Table 20 records percentages for the language variables at the three cluster stage, while Figure 19 shows the location of the wards that fall within each of the resultant groupings. Again the classification is seen to maintain a high degree of spatial cohesion. The two new clusters (clusters 1 and 2) that are distinguished here result from a sub-division of cluster 1, as described above. The classification suggests that within this 'Outer Wales' zone more subtle linguistic differences can be discerned. The first of the new clusters – cluster 1 – includes 419 wards. Together, they delimit a region that embraces the old Marcher territories – south Pembrokeshire, the Gower, the Vale of Glamorgan, the former county of Monmouthshire and the border fringes of Powys and Flintshire. In these areas knowledge of Welsh is seen to be very limited indeed, the percentage of the resident population claiming an ability to speak Welsh being a lowly 11.4. While this is the case, it is worth noting that, collectively and in absolute terms, the wards within this cluster (many of which are densely populated) do

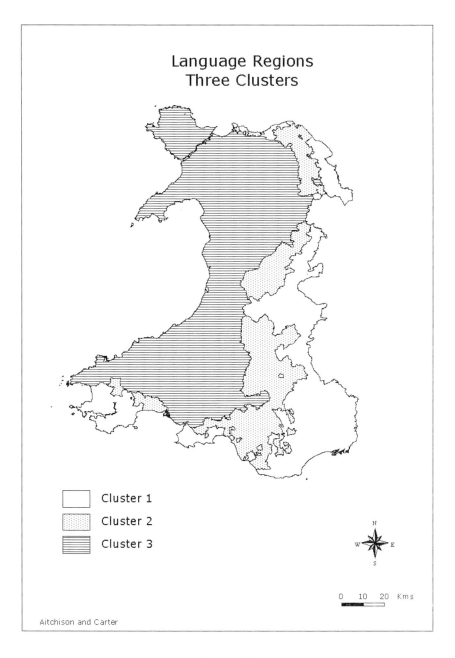

Language Regions
Three Clusters

Cluster 1
Cluster 2
Cluster 3

0   10   20   Kms

Aitchison and Carter

Figure 19.

113

have quite large numbers of resident Welsh-speakers (184,451). Indeed, they account for nearly a third of the total Welsh-speaking population in Wales.

Cluster 2 identifies a zone that is intermediate in nature, both in its linguistic character and its spatial distribution. The 188 wards that make up this cluster lie sandwiched between clusters 1 and 3 (Figure 19) and define a transitional fringe zone around the main Welsh-speaking heartland (Cluster 3). Here knowledge of Welsh is again rather limited. The proportion of the population able to speak Welsh is 16.2. Percentages for the other language indicators are in all cases higher than those for cluster 1. They are, however, much lower than those recorded for cluster 3, the attributes of which were described above under cluster 2 at the two cluster stage.

Interestingly, it might perhaps have been expected that the three cluster stage would demonstrate Balsom's (1985) widely used 'Three Wales' model of *Y Fro Gymraeg*, Welsh Wales and British Wales. But it does not do so, implying that language does not fit easily into that concept, although it was an element in its construction.

Table 20

Language regions – 3 cluster stage

	Cluster 1	Cluster 2	Cluster 3
Number of Wards	419	188	274
% Understand	3.4	6.2	8.2
% Speak only	1.9	2.6	6.2
% Speak/Read	0.8	1.4	3.0
% Speak/Read/Write	8.7	12.2	47.9
% Other Skills	2.5	4.5	2.3
% No Knowledge	82.7	73.1	32.4
Number of Welsh-speakers	184451	90823	300365

(iii) Four cluster stage

The four cluster stage sees the splitting of the main Welsh heartland cluster (cluster 3 in the previous cluster stage) into new groups – clusters 3 and 4. Of these, cluster 3 is the largest, with 177 wards. Figure 20 reveals that these wards form a very compact and extensive region embracing the mainly rural areas of west and north Wales. Here 61.2 per cent of the resident population – 186,874 in total – claims an ability to speak Welsh, while just 30.6 per cent have no knowledge whatsoever of the language (Table 21). At this level of regionalization cluster 3 might be said to define the bounds of *Y Fro Gymraeg*. The cluster that has broken away from this core area – cluster 4 – includes a set of wards, largely located along the south-eastern edge of the region. This zone, which comprises the old industrial areas stretching from Llanelli through to the Aman valley, has long been recognised as being an important region in terms of numbers of Welsh-speakers, but concern has been expressed as to the true strength and quality of the language. This also applies to the other wards in the cluster. These are more scattered in distribution, but they serve to identify further points of weakness within and on the fringes of the essentially rural heartland. The areas concerned include the section of coast between Conwy and Bangor in north Wales, the Conwy valley, the Dolgellau region and small towns along the coast of Ceredigion and north Pembrokeshire – the Penparcau district of Aberystwyth, Aberaeron, Newquay, and Dewisland or the St David's Peninsula.

For the wards in this cluster the proportion of the resident populations aged three and over that can only 'understand' or only 'speak' Welsh is very high at nearly 20 per cent; the proportion able to speak, read and write is consequently much reduced at 35.7 per cent. Despite this, the actual numbers of Welsh-speakers (113,491), and most certainly their density on the ground, is very high. Within the area defined by this cluster are located nearly 20 per cent of all Welsh-speakers. The decline in numbers of Welsh-speakers that has characterised this vulnerable part of south Wales

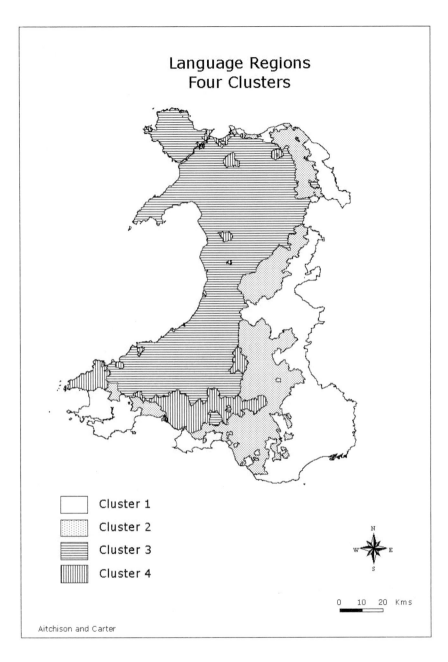

Language Regions
Four Clusters

Cluster 1
Cluster 2
Cluster 3
Cluster 4

0 10 20 Kms

Aitchison and Carter

Figure 20.

in the hinterlands of Llanelli and Ammanford (see above) is evidently of critical significance to the future of the language nationally.

Clusters 1 and 2 remain the same as those identified at the three cluster stage.

Table 21

Language regions – four cluster stage

	Cluster 1	Cluster 2	Cluster 3	Cluster 4
Number of Wards	419	188	177	97
% Understand	3.4	6.2	6.4	11.5
% Speak only	1.9	2.6	5.2	8.0
% Speak/Read	0.8	1.4	2.4	4.2
% Speak/Read/Write	8.7	12.2	53.6	37.6
% Other Skills	2.5	4.5	1.8	3.1
% No Knowledge	82.7	73.1	30.6	35.7
Number of Welsh-speakers	184451	90823	186874	113491

(iv) Five Cluster Stage

The two new clusters at this stage in the regionalization derive from the splitting of a cluster that was first delineated at the three cluster stage (then Cluster 2). This cluster was described as occupying an intermediate position in terms of its linguistic attributes; spatially, it formed a transitional fringe zone around the main heartland core. The sub-division of this cluster yields two distinctive groupings (Clusters 2 and 3). The first, cluster 2, includes 100 wards, the great majority of which form a discrete and compact 'urban' region centred on the local authority areas of Neath, Rhondda Cynon Taf, Bridgend and western parts of the Vale of Glamorgan (Figure 21). A small number of wards within the cluster are to be found in the Wrexham area (Ruabon and Brymbo), in Flintshire (Leeswood) and around

117

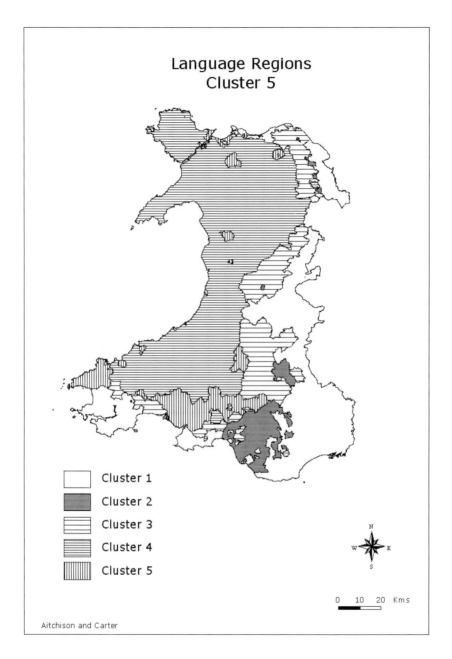

Figure 21.

the town of Brecon in Powys. The cluster is characterized by the high percentage of the population with no knowledge of Welsh (77.9 per cent) and the low proportion of Welsh-speakers – 12.1 (Table 22). Of the five clusters this grouping records the highest proportion – 5.2 per cent – for those having 'other combinations of skills' (e.g. reading and writing, but not speaking Welsh).

The 88 wards that form cluster 3 are mainly located in more rural areas, and take in large parts of western and central Powys, together with eastern Denbighshire and Flintshire. In south Wales a distinctive grouping of wards is identified to the north of Swansea. Cluster 3 is similar in linguistic character to cluster 2, but is seen to contain greater numbers of Welsh-speakers and to display generally higher levels of literacy. Nearly 21 per cent of the population are able to speak Welsh. The proportion of the population indicating that they can 'understand' spoken Welsh only is also quite high (7.8 per cent).

The language profiles of clusters 1, 4 and 5 have already been described at earlier cluster stages.

Table 22

Language regions – five cluster stage

	Cluster 1	Cluster 2	Cluster 3	Cluster 4	Cluster 5
Number of Wards	419	100	88	177	97
% Understand	3.4	4.8	7.8	6.4	11.5
% Speak only	1.9	1.9	3.4	5.2	8.0
% Speak/Read	0.8	1.0	1.9	2.4	4.2
% Speak/Read/Write	8.7	9.2	15.6	53.6	37.6
% Other Skills	2.5	5.2	3.7	1.8	3.1
% No Knowledge	82.7	77.9	67.6	30.6	35.7
Number Welsh-speakers	184451	41656	49167	186874	113491

(v) Six Cluster Stage

The final level of regionalization to be considered here identifies six clusters of wards, and derives from the sub-division of the cluster comprising 177 wards that was first distinguished at the four cluster stage (then Cluster 3). It will be recalled that this cluster included wards located within the main Welsh-speaking heartland. The two new clusters – clusters 4 and 6 – serve to highlight the distinction within this core between those areas where the language still has a very strong hold, and those where it would appear to be weakening. Cluster 6 includes 103 wards and has a total Welsh-speaking population of 113,966 – 19.7 per cent of the all Welsh-speakers (Table 23). The percentage of the resident population able to speak Welsh is the highest of all the clusters – 69.4. Particularly noteworthy is the fact that 62.1 per cent of the population is able to speak, read and write the language. The proportion claiming no knowledge of Welsh is the lowest of all the clusters – 24.1 per cent. Figure 22 indicates that the wards within this cluster dominate in Ynys Môn, the Llŷn Peninsula, the hill areas of central Gwynedd and Denbighshire, and much of Ceredigion. Together, these regions constitute the main stronghold of the language. The 74 wards that comprise cluster 4 are of particular interest for they identify those areas where, although the proportion of the population able to speak Welsh is still relatively high – nearly 50 per cent, so are proportions for those who have no knowledge of Welsh (39.6), and those who claim only to be able to understand the language (8.3 per cent). The regions concerned include a band of wards stretching across north Pembrokeshire and north Carmarthesnhire; and a further band extending down the coast from Llanbedr in Gwynedd to Llanfarian, south of Aberystwyth. Also within this cluster is the set of wards that have long been identified as marking a zone of linguistic fracture in the Snowdonia region. Across the Menai Straits within Ynys Môn a further 11 wards exhibit similar characteristics. Again, this set of wards epitomises the threats to the language which, though varied in nature, illustrate the very real

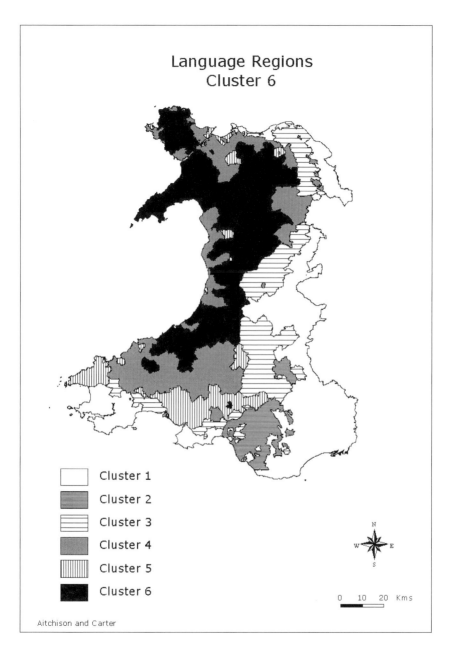

Language Regions
Cluster 6

Cluster 1
Cluster 2
Cluster 3
Cluster 4
Cluster 5
Cluster 6

0   10   20   Kms

Aitchison and Carter

Figure 22.

121

problems for the future.

The attributes of the other clusters recognised at this stage have been described above, and need not be considered further. Overall, the patterns that are displayed at this six cluster stage would appear to offer a concise summary of the linguistic geography of Wales. It draws attention to important regional nuances and differences in terms of knowledge of the language and associated degrees of literacy.

Table 23

Language regions – six cluster stage

	Cluster1	Cluster 2	Cluster 3	Cluster 4	Cluster 5	Cluster 6
Number of Wards	419	100	88	74	97	103
% Understand	3.4	4.8	7.8	8.3	11.5	5.1
% Speak only	1.9	1.9	3.4	5.3	8.0	5.2
% Speak/Read	0.8	1.0	1.9	2.9	4.2	2.1
% Speak/Read/Write	8.7	9.2	15.6	41.7	37.6	62.1
% Other Skills	2.5	5.2	3.8	2.3	3.1	1.4
% No Knowledge	82.7	77.9	67.6	39.6	35.7	24.1
No. Welsh-speakers	184451	41656	49167	72908	113491	113966

7. LANGUAGE, PLACE OF BIRTH AND ETHNICITY

Although not solely or specifically related to the issue of language, it is of interest to consider two other sets of data collated from the 2001 census. The first of these concerns the place of birth of those enumerated. This is of relevance to an analysis of language variations and trends since the movement of people both into and out of Wales clearly impacts on both the absolute and relative strength of the language. This matter has already been addressed within the broader context of population change and migration and need not be elaborated upon further. The second set of data is that derived from responses to the 'ethnic group' question. This question was designed to record each person's perceived ethnic group and cultural background, and to this end respondents were presented with a series of tick boxes. Unfortunately, although in Scotland there was an appropriate box to be ticked, and in England and Wales a box for the Irish, there was no such box for the Welsh. Needless to say, this omission aroused considerable indignation. It certainly fomented fractious debate in the media. In consequence, some people reportedly refused to answer the question, or indeed to complete the census form. The only recourse for those who felt their 'Welshness' strongly enough was to write their ethnicity into the catch-all box labelled 'Any other White background'. The resultant enumerations are inevitably partial, since many will no doubt have failed to appreciate this latter opportunity to express their true sense of identity. For what it is worth (statistically-speaking), the Office for National Statistics has collated these 'write-in' responses, and published the number of persons who specifically declared themselves as 'Welsh'. It

123

is evident that the numbers concerned are much lower than would have been expected if the census form had been properly structured, with a separate box being included for the declaration of a Welsh identity. That said, the pattern of the returns is of interest in its own right, for it is refers to a section of the population that has a manifestly strong sense of its Welshness. Given the close cultural linkage between ethnicity and language, the relationship between the various sets of statistics are also worthy of examination. Significantly, the Office for National Statistics has recently announced (January, 2004) that in future censuses and surveys the ethnic group question will specifically include a 'Welsh' category.

Table 24 records, for local authorities, the number of people born in Wales, and the number who specifically indicated that they were 'Welsh' in the ethnic group question. These are also expressed as percentages of the total populations within the regions concerned. The tabulation shows that just over three-quarters of the resident population (2,188,754) were actually born in Wales. At the local authority level values ranged from a low of 51 per cent (Flintshire) to a high of 91 per cent (Blaenau Gwent). In the old urban and industrial regions of South Wales percentages are generally in excess of 80. In addition to the borderland, where it has been a longstanding process, in-migration has strongly influenced certain areas in north and west Wales. Thus in Conwy, Denbighshire and Ceredigion the proportion of the respective populations born in Wales is less than 60 per cent. As far as the language is concerned the situation in Ceredigion (59 per cent) would appear to be critical. However, as already noted, the figures here are likely to have been heavily affected by the relatively high numbers of non-Welsh students recorded in the university towns of Aberystywth and Lampeter. While this is probably the case, Figure 23, which records percentages at the ward level, does suggest that the relatively low ratios are indeed widespread throughout this particular region. A comparison with the map produced on the same basis for 1991 (Aitchison and Carter, 2000, 110) indicates that in this area the proportion of resident

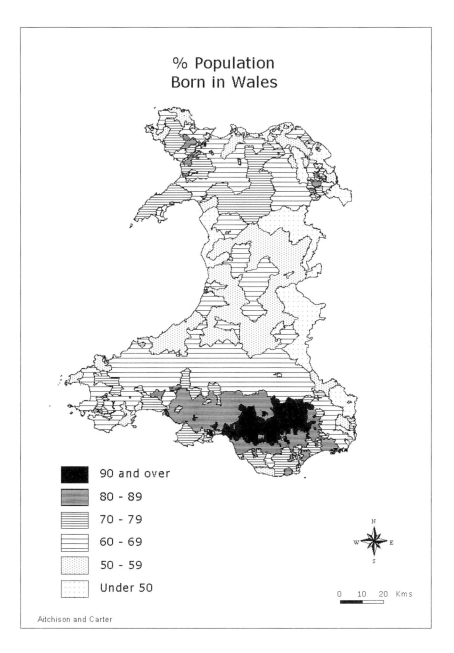

% Population
Born in Wales

90 and over
80 - 89
70 - 79
60 - 69
50 - 59
Under 50

Aitchison and Carter

N
W   E
S

0   10   20   Kms

Figure 23.

125

Table 24

Ethnicity and Place of Birth

Local Authority Area	Number identifying themselves as Welsh	% Population identifying themselves as Welsh	Number Born in Wales	% Population Born in Wales
Blaenau Gwent	8417	12.0	64513	92.1
Brigend	20275	15.8	108952	84.7
Caerphilly	26276	15.5	152462	89.9
Cardiff	40220	13.2	228849	74.9
Carmarthenshire	40471	23.4	138390	80.1
Ceredigion	16307	21.8	43903	58.6
Conwy	13289	12.1	59141	54.0
Denbighshire	9829	10.6	53886	57.9
Flintshire	8662	5.8	75988	51.1
Gwynedd	31356	26.8	81567	69.8
Merthyr Tydfil	9065	16.2	51481	92.0
Monmouthshire	5871	6.9	52031	61.3
Neath/Port Talbot	22872	17.0	120338	89.5
Newport	12326	9.0	111148	81.1
Pembrokeshire	14912	13.1	78434	68.7
Powys	15927	12.6	70238	55.6
Rhondda Cynon Taf	38384	16.5	208567	89.9
Swansea	34135	15.3	183269	82.1
Torfaen	8934	9.8	77788	85.5
Vale of Glamorgan	15252	12.8	90251	75.7
Wrexham	12065	9.4	92399	71.9
Ynys Môn	12975	19.4	45159	67.6
Wales	**417820**	**14.4**	**2188754**	**75.4**

populations born in Wales has declined significantly. Indeed this would appear to apply to much of mid-Wales. Here, many wards record percentages of less than 60. Similar figures are seen to apply in much of the borderland, and in other favoured landscapes such as the National Parks (Snowdonia, Brecon Beacons and Pembrokeshire Coast) and Areas of Outstanding Natural Beauty (e.g. Clwydian Range, Ynys Môn, Gower Pensinsula and the Wye valley). These areas have long been attractive to incomers and second-home owners, and percentages for those born in Wales have generally fallen over the past ten years. Elsewhere, however, it is evident that the situation has remained relatively stable. Perhaps unsurprisingly, the very strong core, centred on the old mining valleys of south Wales, continues to stand out, with percentages of Welsh-born residents exceeding 90.

As to the issue of ethnic identity, Table 24 confirms that, for reasons cited above, a very low number of the resident population in Wales formally declared themselves as being 'Welsh' – 417,820. This amounts to just 14 per cent of the total population. Interestingly, the highest percentages were recorded by local authorities in the main Welsh-speaking heartland areas – Gwynedd (26.8 per cent), Carmarthenshire (23.4 per cent), Ceredigion (21.8 per cent) and Ynys Môn (19.4 per cent). Figure 24 shows that a substantial number of wards within these regions return values generally in excess of 25 per cent. The highest percentages of all are seen to be recorded by a contiguous, and quite extensive, cluster of wards located in the Llŷn Peninsula and in the central hill areas of North Wales; here 'Welsh' percentages are 30 or above. Similar figures apply within a few isolated clusters of wards in the Carmarthenshire region, and in central Ynys Môn. In sharp contrast, beyond these areas, and especially along the borderland fringes, the Vale of Glamorgan and south Pembrokeshire the proportion of resident populations identifying themselves as 'Welsh' is less than 10. Overall, it is apparent that a strong, positive correlation exists between the percentage of people within a locality who speak Welsh and the proportion who claimed a Welsh identity. Finally, it is worth observing that, while 'Welsh' percentages for local authorities across much of South Wales are generally close to the national average, the absolute numbers involved are actually relatively high (e.g. Cardiff (40,222), Rhondda Cynon Taf (38,384) and Swansea (34,135).

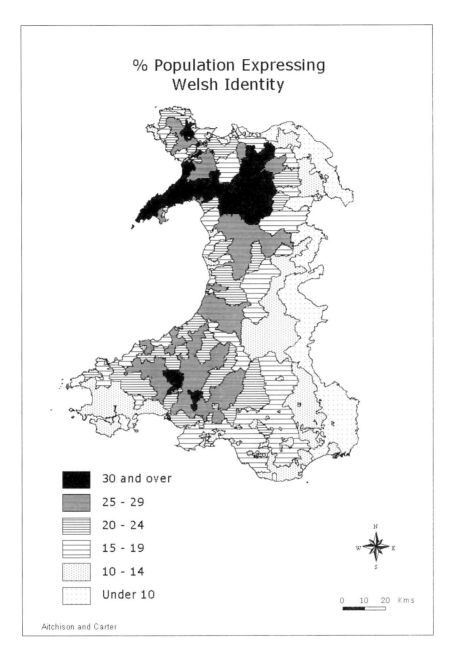

% Population Expressing
Welsh Identity

30 and over
25 - 29
20 - 24
15 - 19
10 - 14
Under 10

N
W E
S

0   10   20   Kms

Aitchison and Carter

Figure 24.

129

8. SUMMARY REVIEW

Before moving on to reflect on the implications of the various findings derived from the 2001 census a brief synopsis is in order, if only to distil the essential lines of argument. There is a danger of laboured repetition in so doing, but the discussion has ranged very widely indeed and in places has been complex – perhaps even to the point of confusion, given the deluge of data that has been presented. A number of general observations are worth re-iterating. Firstly, it is evident that as far as the linguistic landscape of Wales is concerned there still exists a core or heartland of predominantly Welsh speech. In comparison with the situation prevailing in the not too distant past, however, it is greatly attenuated in geographical extent and impaired in its internal structure. It is a relict element of a once much larger '*Bro Gymraeg*'. This core is surrounded, and partly interpenetrated, by those areas which were formerly part of it, but which have now fallen away. Here only just over 50 per cent of the population is able to speak Welsh and a large section have no skills in the language. They constitute those areas where Anglicization, partly linked to tourism and the attraction of the environment to incomers, has reduced the integrity of identity. Among them is the distinctive break line across Snowdonia from Conwy to Porthmadog – a line that takes in two settlements that have become key centres of tourism and recreation – Betws-y-Coed and Capel Curig. Other zones of fracture are the coastal fringes of Meirionnydd and Ceredigion, as well as those of Ynys Môn. But undoubtedly the area that should be the cause of greatest concern is that of the industrial south-west, the former anthracite mining and tinplate producing areas of what were formerly east Carmarthenshire and west Glamorgan. Here language decline is evidenced by the catastrophic collapse in numbers and proportions between 1991 and 2001. The word 'catastrophic' is used because in this area, where there are still large populations of Welsh-speakers, there seems no obvious reason for the decline. Because of its significance in language numbers and the problems it presents, this area was included in *The Community Research Project* by the Welsh Language Board (Williams and Evas, 1997). Two parts were selected for review, Cwm Gwendraeth and Cwm Aman. In Cwm Gwendraeth 'significant and strong support' was found for the language and it was found that 'the family unit operates as an effective agency of language transmission' (pp14/15). There was 'a reliable process of intergenerational language transmission' and 'a great potential for the future of Welsh in Cwm Gwendraeth' (p17). Even so, in the inter-censal period 1991 to 2001 the percentage speaking Welsh in Gorslas fell from 78.4 to 70.4 and in Pontyberem from 80.5 to 73.3. The necessary reservations must be made as to the comparison of census data between the two dates, but the figures do not seem to bear out the sanguine view expressed in the survey. The authors were less optimistic in their findings in Cwm Aman reporting that the family unit was a much less efficient agent of language transmission (p17), and that there was a significant erosion of the language in the Aman Valley as a result of that and of the 'out-migration of young people' (p18). But the census returns for the Aman valley reveal a situation not greatly different from that in Cwm Gwendraeth. The percentage of Welsh-speakers fell from 70.8 to 62.0 in Ammanford and from 77.0 to 67.1 in Glanamman. Unless out-migration is language specific, and there is no evidence that it is, it is difficult to see how deindustrialization and out-migration can of themselves affect the proportion of Welsh-speakers in an area. What is puzzling, and it is attested by the lower proportion in the younger age groups with the ability to speak Welsh, is the apparent failure of transmission within families. It stands in direct contrast to the pattern in areas of language growth and seems at odds with the strong attachment to things Welsh in the area. It is all the more understandable therefore that the earliest '*mentrau iaith*' initiatives were located in this part of Wales. But it is as if the conditions and the attitudes of the inter-war period still operate in the area; it seems to lag in the past. Maybe the area is just too far removed from the dynamic of growth in the service occupations which has suffused the south-east, producing reactions which make the area appear as a backwater lacking the investment and excitement of more advantaged areas in the hinterland of Cardiff. It is to be hoped that the developments taking place in Swansea and on the coastal belt about Llanelli will generate a revived commitment to language and culture. But given their history and place in Welsh life it is difficult to see why the Aman Valley and Cwm Gwendraeth should not be power centres in language regeneration. The low levels of literacy and the age structure of the Welsh-speaking population are no doubt relevant, but there must be more to it than that, for they are no more than evidence of the underlying problem.

Outside these old language cores the marcher lands have demonstrated strong growth, though throughout the analysis this has always been qualified by reference to very low starting bases. Much of the increase has been amongst the young and there perhaps the problem lies, for although claims to speak Welsh may be made in the census form as a result of school instruction, the real depth of the language within society can be questioned. Undoubtedly the movement of Welsh-speakers from the heartland, a migratory flow which is often overlooked, for it is also responsible for loss in that heartland, has contributed greatly to the increase. The children of such migrants educated through the medium of Welsh, and speaking some Welsh at home, could well make a more lasting and basic contribution to the language in these marcher territories.

It is evident from the evaluation of the various language indicators presented here that the linguistic landscape of Wales continues to be fashioned by competing, and often contradictory, forces. While the basic data confirm that very significant advances have been made over the past decade, it is also possible to raise doubts and questions as to their meaningfulness in the long term. That this is the case has been intimated at various points in the discussion thus far. It also opens up a much wider debate concerning what is needed to sustain – in the words (quoted at the outset) of Saunders Lewis – a truly 'living language'.

The Future of the Welsh Language : Some Reflections

One overriding conclusion emerges from this analysis of the 2001 census. It is that the trends exhibited in immediately previous decades have continued. The traditional heartland of the language has suffered further erosion, and gains have been recorded in those parts long regarded as Anglicized. This immediately triggers the question as to how this process, seemingly now well established and giving no indication of modification, will condition the future of Welsh. Over the past decade the notion of 'language death' has attracted considerable interest within the academic literature. So much so, that a virtual eschatology of languages has been built up as the processes of decay and extinction have been traced. Within this body of literature there is a high degree of agreement on the basic track to extinction and there is no great subtlety in the arguments that have been proffered. Decline, it is argued, is brought about by the impinging on a lesser-used language of a major world language, or even a more powerful language in that it is spoken by a larger number of people and is equated with economic advantage and associated with social and political power. There is a gradual transition as the stronger language is adopted until the lesser language is ousted. The internal linguistic processes are articulated in the concepts of code mixing and code switching. In the first, vocabulary from the more powerful language penetrates that of the minor language so that sentences contain a mixture of languages, whilst in the second speakers switch from the lesser to the dominant language, initially on more formal occasions. But the process eventually works its way through all the domains of speech so that change, evident at first in formal and public domains such as government, administration and business, becomes completed as the more private domains are invaded. The use of the word 'invaded' suggests a comparison with the sociological concept of invasion and succession used in the penetration of one community's space by another. It is certainly an analogous process, but manifestly one that is very different in its time span. Language invasion is not an immediate process, some languages have been under threat for over a thousand years yet still survive. And just as invasions of space have been physically resisted, so too opposition to linguistic invasion has been characteristic. There are also, of course, structural changes, such as atrophied vocabulary and the death of inflections (McWhorter, 2002, 262–3), again strongly resisted by language purists.

Given the ubiquity of language death – it has been estimated that 'about half the known languages of the world have vanished in the last five hundred years' (Nettle and Romain, 2000, 2) – so there is also a received wisdom as to how resistance can be maintained. It is argued by many that a language can only survive if it has a clear base, a domestic or community base, where it is the first and hence dominant language and literally the mother tongue. That base is usually geographical or spatial in that it forms a distinctive region within a larger territory of lesser use. The children brought up in such an environment preserve the integrity of the language and form a crucial reservoir of speakers. This is also the basis of the standard belief that only through the passing on of language from mother to children can a language survive. 'It is a central tenet of the language-revival movement that a language is only truly alive when it is regularly passed on to children' (McWhorter, 2002, 278). Those children might be dispersed in later life, but they carry the language with them. These language bases act therefore as a core reserve sending out pulses of speakers which keep the language alive over a broader territory. This condition assumes that the core, if not monolingual, returns proportions of speakers well over 70 per cent, and preferably over 80. A condition where those proportions are substantially lowered, even though there is a wider spread bilingualism with proportions nearer 50 per cent, can be interpreted as no more than a stage in language death. Without the resource of first language speakers brought up in the minority language in a well-delineated heartland, then gradual decline and elimination is certain. This is the issue of prime concern to many language activists who see the decline in the Welsh heartland as the greatest threat to the language, and to which the increase in more peripheral areas is no compensation. The evidence from the 2001 census that has been explored here would probably give little comfort to such people, and the decline in the number of wards where over 80 per cent of the population speak Welsh to a figure of only 17, representing only 4.2 per cent of Welsh-speakers, would be seen as especially menacing.

It is apparent also that the conditions of the contemporary world make the sustaining of a territorial power base of lesser-used language communities less and less likely. The critical condition for survival in the past was isolation. That is, the existence of a base into which the penetration of a more powerful language is restricted. But such restriction has been undermined by the technology and mobility of the post-modern world. World languages easily and effectively penetrate the most private of domains, those of family and household. In this regard the all-enveloping presence of the Internet is becoming ever more influential. In addition, increased mobility means that populations now move across the world with ease. Communities can no longer exist in a state of physical and cultural isolation. It is hardly surprising therefore that 'migration' should have become one of the dominant features, indeed one of the dominant controversies, of the twenty-first century. Even the most powerful of cultures have become agitated over the impact of immigrants upon identity and values. Political correctness has sought solution, or amelioration, in the notion of multiculturalism. But lack of assimilation brings with it the danger, if that be a proper term, of isolated linguistic and cultural enclaves within a country. Learning and adopting the language of the receiving country is seen as a necessity for in-migrants.

The reactions of lesser-used languages to the two types of threat, those from loss of isolation and from the impact of in-migration, have been clear in intent, if not in detailed action. Thus, in Wales there has been a continued concern with both technological and physical invasion. The penetration by the mass media has been met by the establishment of Welsh language counterparts. Radio Cymru and S4C (Sianel Pedwar Cymru or Channel Four Wales) have attempted to offset the impact of English language radio and television, whilst a number of journals, such as *Barn* and *Golwg* along with *papurau bro* or local Welsh language papers, have provided printed material. The publication of Welsh books, under the auspices of the Welsh Books Council, has also made great progress.

The response to physical mobility, in the form of both the out-migration of Welsh-speakers and the in-migration of monoglot English-speakers, has been much more controversial and much less successful. The basic reaction has been again the obvious one of attempting to preserve Welsh-language communities, both by the retention of native speakers and the minimising of in-migration. But this has had to be conducted in the most unfavourable of economic circumstances. The traditional communities were essentially agricultural and the problems of agriculture, and especially the fall in employment, have undermined their *raison d'être*. The economic bases of these communities have been completely transformed and any notion of restoration into a former condition is totally unreal. It is this situation which makes the safeguarding of Welsh-language communities so difficult, for a whole new economic system is emerging which is not necessarily supportive of the language. Indeed many of the activities now encouraged, for example in tourism, appear to be particularly attractive to immigrants (Phillips and Thomas, 2001). As already indicated, the evidence from the 2001 census tends to show that little success has been demonstrated in these fields, at least as measured by the number of communities where over 80 per cent of the population speak Welsh. From the analyses of change which have been presented here the conclusions are unmistakable.

If the language is crucially, indeed wholly, dependent on the core Welsh-speaking communities of what is regarded as the heartland of the language then the future is bleak. The whole array of measures which are proposed, largely related to economic regeneration and housing, can only have a marginal and belated effect on the remaining communities. Ironically, some of that regeneration may depend on the entrepreneurial spirit and wealth of incomers, and the jobs retained and created by them. That is perhaps a harsh judgement, but it is difficult to see even the most stringent of measures having a significant effect at this stage, and the political possibilities of such measures are certainly limited.

This situation poses two crucial questions which the 2001 census makes more pertinent. Can a language survive without such a core region of first language speakers where it is the mother tongue, a veritable '*Fro Gymraeg*'? Is a widespread bilingualism nothing more than a stage in the process of decline and death? On the answers to these questions rests the future of the language. Given these considerations, then the assumption of the crucial necessity of a core area in geographical terms and the process of transmission within the family in social terms needs to be critically examined; for if they are to become less realisable under post-modern conditions, then language decline and ultimate death are more likely.

It is useful to begin such an examination with two quotations, the first is reproduced by Nettle and Romain in their book *Vanished Voices* (2000), the second is from McWhorter in his book *The Power of Babel* (2002).

'A language cannot be saved by singing a few songs or having a word on a postage stamp. It cannot even be saved by getting "official status" for it, or getting it taught in schools. It is saved by its use (no matter how imperfectly), by its introduction and use in every walk of life and at every conceivable opportunity until it becomes a natural thing, no longer laboured or false. It means in short a period of struggle and hardship. There is no easy route to the restoration of language' (Ellis and mac a'Ghobhain, 1971)

'Yet it is conceivable that languages such as Irish, Welsh, Maori and Hawaiian could be passed on as second languages, taught in school and spoken non-natively but proficiently, *in perpetuo*. Under such conditions, the languages could persist as cultural indicators, the very learning of the language in school itself constituting a hallmark of cultural identity… It is perhaps something of a western conceit to suppose that a language is not "a language" unless it is spoken from the cradle… For better or for worse, the cultural conditions are present to preserve, for example, Irish within what could be considered a domain for minority languages commensurate with new world conditions: a living taught language. (McWhorter, 2001, 279).

From these two quotations some crucial arguments can be distilled. The first is that widespread use is an imperative if a language is to survive. A language confined to limited and possibly peripheral areas of a country has little hope of development. More likely, it will exist as an isolated 'ghetto' which will slowly attenuate and decline. Even if it does survive, a character as some quaint representative of a past but no longer very relevant to the future, is hardly one to be contemplated with satisfaction.

The second argument is epitomised in one sentence from McWhorter – 'languages could persist as cultural indicators'. This also appears in a similar form in Crystal – 'a view of language as a pre-eminent but not exclusive badge of ethnicity provides the most promising basis for the maintenance of an endangered language' (Crystal, 2000, 122). Crystal's qualification, 'but not exclusive', can be noted and treated later. The vitality of a language rests upon three bases which can be thought of as a three-legged stool. The first of them is status, for it is necessary for a language to have an effective social status backed by a clear legal status for it to thrive. The second is economic status, for if a language is seen as of little value then the incentive to reproduce it, to retain or learn it, is threatened. The third is ethnic identity, the close association of the language with ethnicity which gives strength and meaning to the population speaking the language, a badge of significance and belonging. The analogy of a three-legged stool is relevant in that all three bases are closely related, so much so that without one the whole structure is in danger of collapse.

The Policy Review of the Welsh Language – *Our Language : Its Future* (The National Assembly for Wales, 2002) – can be considered against the background which has been sketched above, and mainly through an analysis of the Summary of Recommendations. Many of these can be termed 'mechanistic' in that they are primarily concerned with the establishment of the mechanisms for the promotion of the language. This is not in any way to denigrate them, for they are basic to the language's future. But they are not directly related to the concerns which have been discussed here. Of this operational nature are all those matters concerned with *Mentrau Iaith*, language initiatives within communities (Williams, 1999), and indeed, the whole of Part 2 of the Summary, the recommendations of the Education and Lifelong Learning Committee. Many of the other statements are those of general principle – 'The Assembly should provide leadership in developing a bilingual Wales' (p.7). These are unexceptional and in a document of this nature, wholly appropriate. But the central and crucial concern is, however, the way in which the Committee responds to the more controversial, and in that sense the more critical, matters relating to the language.

There are three language issues which arouse the greatest controversy. These are the nature of support to be given to the Welsh-speaking communities of the language heartland, the need for revision of the Welsh Language Act of 1993, and the association of ethnic identity with language. On all these the Policy Review takes the most conservative of attitudes and moves away from any statement of a fundamental nature. Thus, although there is a great deal about support of communities and invocation of planning decisions, and much of a very general and obvious character, the basic need to consider language as crucial in housing, for example, is overtly rejected. 'Local Authorities should be encouraged to use all the powers available to them, including housing and planning powers, to enable local people to secure homes, either by purchase or rent, within their own community, but that in the exercise of these powers, there shall be no discrimination on the basis of language' (p.11). Again, a negative reaction is advanced in relation to any need for modification of the Language Act. 'The 1993 Act should be used as fully as the powers in it permit, so that the limits of those powers are reached before any comprehensive legislation is sought' (p13). A sentence which neatly illustrates an official way of rejection, without being clear and firm and open in that decision. The third of the issues, that of the relation of language to ethnic identity, is also fraught with difficulties. Unfortunately, owing to the insensitivity of the Office of National Statistics, and its subsequent intransigence, the census data on ethnic identity were completely compromised. Even so, the crucial problem is the need to create an association between being Welsh and speaking Welsh, for only with that firmly established is there real hope for the emergence of a truly bilingual Wales to replace the old polarised split between a Welsh-Wales and an Anglo-Wales. But that creates real problems for both the Assembly and the Welsh Language Board, problems which like those relating to housing and a language law are seen as better set aside. The two main problems related to the association of language and ethnic identity are first the alienation of the predominant non-Welsh-speaking section of the population on whose good will much of the progress made in language retention has been dependent, and second in the necessary genuflection to multiculturalism which political correctness demands. Even so, on the path toward a realistic bilingualism the issue will have to be faced, for without that conviction a prime element in motivation will be missing. Moreover there is a well recognised and growing threat from an institutional basis of identity based on a whole range of elements other than language.

The core of this problem is, of course, one of the oldest and longest standing of questions in the field of ethnic studies, the characteristics which make up an ethnic identity. The notion of nationalism in this context can be set aside, for the bases of political separation constitute a related but separate issue (Williams, 1982, 1997). Even so, the definition of ethnicity is itself complex. Anthony D. Smith writes, 'ethnicity is largely "mythic" and "symbolic" in character, and because myths and symbols, memories and values are "carried" in and by forms and genres of artefacts and activities which change only very slowly, so *ethnie*, once formed, tends to be exceptionally durable under "normal" vicissitudes and to persist over many generations, even centuries, forming "moulds" within which all kinds of social and cultural processes can unfold and upon which all kinds of circumstances and pressures can exert an impact' (Smith, 1986, 16). That is a view which can be accepted. Indeed, appropriately, it is very close to standard definitions of culture. But the critical problem is to identify the carriers of the myths, symbols, memories and values, and to evaluate contemporary modifications and the circumstances which generate them. Put simply, the question that needs to be addressed is, 'What are the defining characters of Welshness?'. In response, and set against the quotation from Smith, there are two contrasting positions.

The first is that subscribed to by language activists. Their argument is based on the fact that Wales has never had a true political unity due to its very early assimilation by England, certainly two centuries before either Ireland or Scotland. Thus none of the trappings of modern identity in the legal or governmental context of the nation state ever developed. Such as there were, for example a separate legal system, were snuffed out at the so-called Act of Union of 1536 and the Act of Great Sessions of 1543. Wales lost all the formal institutions about which identity can gather. One thing alone remained, one carrier of the myths, symbols and values, and that was the language. It is only language, and the culture derived from it and associated with it, that distinguishes a Welsh person from a provincial English person. Thus, for example, one of the core factors in any ethnic identity is the body of literature built up over centuries and carrying the myths and traditions in the most tangible form. But if a person living in Wales can only read English then the basic orientation will be toward the identity symbolised by that language rather than to a Welshness derived from a Welsh literary heritage, whatever the strength of an Anglo-Welsh literature. At this point, too, it is worth observing that in the attempt to define identity through markers other than language, the characteristics of the mining valleys of South Wales are often converted into an epitome of Welshness. But apart from its regional limitation, most of the features – the closeness of communities, the radicalism of politics, the nonconformity, the distinctive choral tradition, even the commitment to rugby football – are not of anything distinctively Welsh, but of societies distinctively industrial. It is certainly possible to match each of the features in the north of England and, indeed, *mutatis mutandi*, in any mining community across the world. What was distinctive about South Wales in the crucial phase of its development was the Welsh language; Gwyn A. Williams argued that Merthyr Tydfil was the first Welsh town.

The view of the primacy of the language is well set out by Ned Thomas when he writes that Welsh 'carries a symbolic charge out of all proportion to that which one expects to find in every language alongside its function as a tool of communication. There is something ultimately mysterious, because unconscious, in this clinging to the language. It is a question of holding on to an identity…' (Thomas, 1971, 39). That 'holding on' is all the more crucial since all the other symbols of identity were either stripped away following the assimilation of Wales into England, or are not uniquely distinctive of Wales.

The second of the two positions on the identity issue is radically different, and is raised in the conclusion to the quotation from Thomas in the preceding paragraph… 'and if this identity were able to flower in other ways, say through political control of our own future, the language would probably not continue to carry the high symbolic charge it carries

142

now' (Thomas, 1971, 39). It was also partly surmised by Saunders Lewis in 1962 when he wrote, *'Yn fy marn i, pe ceid unrhyw fath o hunan lywodraeth i Gymru cyn arddel ar arfer yr iaith Gymraeg yn iaith swyddogol yn holl weinyddiad yr awdurdodau lleol a gwladol yn y rhanbarthau Cymraeg o'n wlad, ni cheid mohoni'n iaith swyddogol o gwbl, a byddai tranc yr iaith yn gynt nag y bydd ei thranc hi dan lywodraeth Loegr'* (Lewis, 1962, 30). ('In my opinion, if any kind of self-government for Wales were obtained before the Welsh language was acknowledged and used as an official language in local authority and state administration in the Welsh-speaking parts of our country, then the language would never achieve official status at all, and its demise would be quicker than it will be under English rule') (Jones and Thomas, 1973, 141). Modern Welsh nationalism, carrying with it a sense of ethnic difference, dates from the marked revival which took place at the end of the nineteenth century. From it there developed a series of institutions, the University of Wales, the National Library, the National Museum, all of which symbolised and proclaimed a new-found identity. The argument of those who deny the sole and central role of language is based on the development of this institutional base. The second half of the last century witnessed the creation of the Welsh Office and the devolution of a significant sector of government to its control. The Welsh Assembly, which met first in 1999, is a substantial step further. In this way, and through institutions which are specifically Welsh, a sense of identity is building up which is unrelated to language. Again, the late nineteenth century also saw the development of Welsh sports teams, especially in rugby (Smith and Williams, 1980), and these, too, projected a Welshness which was independent of language. It can, therefore, be contended that Wales is developing a sense of identity reliant on national institutions more akin to other former colonial territories where, although English might be the predominant language, identity does not depend on it. Australia, even the USA, can be cited as examples, but so too can the Celtic countries nearer home. Scottish ethnic identity is only tenuously linked to Gaelic speech; much more important are its distinctive legal and educational systems. Even in Ireland the prime place of the language is more notional than real. There are in Welsh society, it can be contended, profound internal divisions based on ethnicity, language and class. But much of the division can be side-tracked by eliminating the issue of language and building on the elaboration of institutions and other elements about which a collective sense of identity can develop. The clear implication is that in this way Welsh identity could be advanced, with feelings of association and belonging becoming much more inclusive and universal.

These polarised notions of the cultural or institutional bases of identity have been widely discussed in relation to nationalisms. But manifestly in reality they are not sharply and irreconcilably opposed. As Anthony D. Smith writes, 'any *ethnie*, then, that aspires to nationhood must become political and stake out claims in the competition for power and influence in the state arena' (Smith, 1986, 156). That is, it must become a protagonist in the formation, promotion and operation of representative institutions. Likewise, those committed primarily to the development of 'national' institutions can see in them and their role the strongest means of support for the language and the culture it embodies. The two extremes merge and are combined in various degrees of priority by Welsh people.

Even so, if what has happened in Wales over the last thirty years is reviewed, then it becomes evident that the first of the two views set out above, that the language is the predominant marker of being Welsh, has generally dominated. Language activists have seized the high ground in the contention over what constitutes Welshness, largely by commanding the sources of power over opinion. On this much of the success has depended. But even so, the evidence presented here would suggest that major problems remain. However effective local initiatives might be, the overarching success in the promotion of the language can only be achieved by convincing all of the people of the centrality of the association of Welsh identity with the language. Perhaps this is no more than a major marketing exercise. The policy statement by the Welsh Assembly Government was entitled *'A Bilingual Future'*, and it there states that the Assembly, through the Welsh Language Board, 'will market and promote the language in all aspects of Welsh life' (Welsh Assembly Government, 2002, 20). That marketing, based on driving forward the conviction that all Welsh people should have some ability in the language, is crucial to the future. In this regard the results of 2001 census are clearly encouraging. The headline statistics confirm the predictions of growth made nearly fifteen years ago, and this in itself is in part a tribute to the Welsh Language Board's efforts. The increase that has been registered nationally in the number of Welsh-speakers should be a cause for considerable satisfaction and hope for the future; but as we have endeavoured to demonstrate here there are still important, and extremely challenging, issues that need to be addressed.

REFERENCES

Aitchison, J.W. and Carter, H. (1985) *The Welsh Language 1961–1981. An Interpretative Atlas.* Cardiff, University of Wales Press.

Aitchison, J.W. and Carter, H. (1985) *The Welsh Language in Cardiff : a quiet revolution.* Transactions of the Institute of British Geographers, new series, 12, 482–92.

Aitchison, J.W. and Carter, H. (1994) *A Geography of the Welsh Language 1961–1991.* Cardiff, University of Wales Press.

Aitchison, J.W. and Carter, H. (1991) Rural Wales and the Welsh Language. *Rural History* 2, 59–76.

Aitchison, J.W. and Carter, H. (2000) *Language, Economy and Society. The Changing Fortunes of the Welsh language in the Twentieth Century.* Cardiff, University of Wales Press.

Aitchison, J.W. and Carter, H. (2000) The Welsh Language 1921–1991. A Geolinguistic Perspective. In Jenkins and Williams edit. Op cit.

Arnold, M. (1867) *Lectures on the Study of Celtic Literature.* London.

Balsom, D. (1985) The three Wales model, in J. Osmond ed. *The National Question Again? Welsh Political Identity in the 1980s.* Llandysul, Gwasg Gomer

Blackaby, D., Murphy, P., O'Leary, N. and Thomas, E. (1995) Wales : an economic survey. *Contemporary Wales*, 8, 213–295

Brooksbank, D. (2002) The Welsh economy : a statistical profile. *Contemporary Wales*, 15, 111–137.

Crystal, D. (2000) *Language Death.* Cambridge, University of Cambridge Press.

Davies, N. (1999) *The Isles : A History.* London, Macmillan

Ellis, P. and mac a'Ghobhainn, S. (1971) *The Problem of Language Revival.* Inverness, Club Leabhar.

Fishlock, T. (1972) *Wales and the Welsh.* London, Cassell.

Giggs, J. and Pattie, E. (1991) Croeso I Gymru. Welcome to Wales, But welcome to whose Wales?. Nottingham, Department of Geography Working Paper. University of Nottingham.

Hughes, H. (1998) *An Uprooted Community. A History of Epynt.* Llandysul, Gwasg Gomer

Jenkins, D. (1998) *A Nation on Trial. Penyberth 1936.* Trans A. Corbett. Cardiff, Welsh Academic Press.

Jenkins, G.H. and Williams, M. (2000*) 'Let's Do Our Best for the Ancient Tongue. The Welsh Language in the Twentieth Century.*Cardiff, University of Wales Press.

Jones, A.R. and Thomas, G. (1973) *Presenting Saunders Lewis.* Cardiff, University of Wales Press

Jones, I.G. (1992) *Mid–Victorian Wales : The Observer and the Observed.* Cardiff, University of Wales Press.

Kearney, H. (1988) *Nineteenth century Britain; Integration and Diversity.* Oxford, Oxford University Press.

Lang, G.E. and Lang, K. (1983) *The Battle for Public Opinion : The President, the Press and the Polls during Watergate.* New York, Columbia University Press.

Lewis, S. (1962) *Tynged yr Iaith.* London, BBC.

Lewis, T. (1926) Sur la distribution du parler Gallois dans le Pays de Galles d'apres le recensement de 1921. *Annales de Geographie,* 1926, 413.

McCombs, M. and Shaw, D. (1972) The agenda setting function of the mass media. Public Opinion Quarterly, 36, 176–187

McWhorter, J. (2002) *The Power of Babel. A Natural History of Language.* London, William Heinemann.

Mitchell, D. (1995) There's no such thing as culture : towards a reconceptualization of the idea of culture in geography. *Trans. of the Institute of British Geographers.* New Series 20 (1), 102–116.

National Assembly for Wales, Culture Committee. (2002) *Our Language : Its Future. Policy Review of the Welsh Language.* Cardiff, National Assembly for Wales.

Nelde, P., Strubell, M. and Williams, G. (1996) *The Production and Reproduction*

147

of Minority Language Groups in the European Union. Luxembourg, Office for the Official Publications of the European Communities.

Nettle, D. and Romain, S. (2000) *Vanishing Voices. The Extinction of the World's Languages*. Oxford, Oxford University Press.

Phillips, D. and Thomas, C. ((2001) *The Effects of Tourism on the Welsh Language in North-West Wales*. Aberystwyth, University of Wales, Centre for Advanced Welsh and Celtic Studies.

Robbins, K.G. (2003) Wales and the 'British Question'. *Transactions of the Honourable Society of Cymmrodorion* New Series 9, 152–161

Smith, A.D. (1986) *The Ethnic Origins of Nations*. Oxford, Blackwell.

Smith, D. and Williams, S. G. (1980*) Fields of Praise. The Official History of the Welsh Rugby Union 1881–1981*. Cardiff, University of Wales Press for the Welsh Rugby Union.

Stevens, C. (1996) *Meithrin. Hanes Mudiad Ysgolion Meithrin*. Llandysul, Gwasg Gomer

Thomas, N. *The Welsh Extremist. A Culture in Crisis*. London, Victor Gollancz Ltd.

Tudur, G. (1989) *Wyt Ti'n Cofio? Chwarter Canrif o Frwydr yr Iaith*, Talybont, Y Lolfa.

Welsh Assembly Government. (2002) *Bilingual Future. Dydfodol Dwyieithog*. Cardiff.

Welsh Language Board. (1996) *A Strategy for the Welsh Language*. Cardiff, Welsh Office. (1997) Digest of Welsh Statistics, Cardiff, Welsh Office.

Williams, C. ed. (1982) *National Separatism*. Cardiff, University of Wales Press.

Williams, C. (1997) *Called unto Liberty. On Language and Nationalism*. Clevedon, Multilingual Matters.

Williams, C.H. and Evas, J (1997) *The Community Research Project*. Cardiff, Bwrdd yr Iaith Gymraeg

Williams, C.H. (1999) Governance and the language. *Contemporary Wales*, 12, 130–154.

Williams, G.A. (1979) *When was Wales?* London, BBC.

APPENDIX

Number and Percentage of Welsh-speakers by Census Ward (Electoral Division) : 2001

Blaenau Gwent

Abertillery	430	9.9
Badminton	268	8.7
Beaufort	417	11.1
Blaina	459	9.8
Brynmawr	487	9.0
Cwm	390	9.3
Cwmtillery	429	9.3
Ebbw Vale North	357	7.8
Ebbw Vale South	335	8.2
Georgetown	312	9.2
Llanhilleth	392	8.5
Nantyglo	373	9.0
Rassau	262	8.2
Sirhowy	507	9.5
Six Bells	227	8.9
Tredegar Central and West	496	8.5

Bridgend

Aberkenfig	174	8.9
Bettws	169	8.6
Blackmill	228	10.1
Blaengarw	179	9.9
Brackla	1065	11.1
Bryncethin	160	12.8
Bryncoch	148	8.4
Bryntirion, Laleston and Merthyr Mawr	443	10.7
Caerau	622	9.2
Cefn Cribwr	139	9.3
Cefn Glas	152	9.0
Coity	149	11.0
Cornelly	622	10.8
Coychurch Lower	134	11.4
Felindre	247	9.8

Hendre	394	10.9
Litchard	252	11.5
Llangeinor	130	11.6
Llangewydd and Brynhyfryd	288	11.1
Llangynwyd	380	13.8
Maesteg East	562	11.6
Maesteg West	768	13.6
Morfa	436	10.6
Nant-y-moel	179	8.1
Newcastle	492	10.0
Newton	335	9.9
Nottage	338	10.4
Ogmore Vale	253	8.3
Oldcastle	579	12.7
Pendre	199	9.9
Penprysg	391	12.9
Pen-y-fai	254	12.3
Pontycymmer	270	11.3
Porthcawl East Central	267	8.3
Porthcawl West Central	343	10.2
Pyle	703	10.1
Rest Bay	222	9.8
Sarn	219	9.2
Ynysawdre	270	9.4

Caerphilly

Aber Valley	994	15.5
Aberbargoed	314	9.2
Abercarn	404	8.7
Argoed	283	11.8
Bargoed	573	9.5
Bedwas, Trethomas and Machen	1120	11.2
Blackwood	828	10.5
Cefn Fforest	371	10.7

149

	Welsh-speakers No. %			Welsh-speakers No. %	
Crosskeys	277	9.2	Llanrumney	789	7.3
Crumlin	551	10.0	Pentwyn	1189	8.5
Darren Valley	270	11.0	Pentyrch	640	18.6
Gilfach	196	9.7	Penylan	1359	12.0
Hengoed	516	10.7	Plasnewydd	1711	10.7
Llanbradach	502	11.3	Pontprennau/		
Maesycwmmer	194	9.3	Old St. Mellons	700	9.2
Morgan Jones	857	13.6	Radyr	683	15.2
Moriah	523	11.9	Rhiwbina	1375	12.6
Nelson	483	10.9	Riverside	1556	13.5
New Tredegar	329	6.9	Rumney	703	8.1
Newbridge	505	8.7	Splott	1026	8.9
Pengam	408	11.1	Trowbridge	1239	8.9
Penmaen	430	10.0	Whitchurch		
Penyrheol	1424	12.9	and Tongwynlais	1991	13.2
Pontllanfraith	698	9.3			
Pontlottyn	119	6.8	**Carmarthenshire**		
Risca East	744	12.1	Abergwili	1267	57.9
Risca West	460	9.3	Ammanford	1599	62.1
St. Cattwg	874	12.2	Betws	1118	62.8
St. James	617	10.9	Bigyn	1745	28.6
St. Martins	886	12.6	Burry Port	1492	36.4
Twyn Carno	245	10.7	Bynea	1067	35.9
Ynysddu	390	11.0	Carmarthen Town		
Ystrad Mynach	440	11.2	North	2085	41.1
			Carmarthen Town		
Cardiff			South	1533	44.5
Adamsdown	591	8.9	Carmarthen Town		
Butetown	358	8.3	West	1813	43.2
Caerau	876	9.0	Cenarth	1161	59.6
Canton	1941	15.4	Cilycwm	694	49.3
Cathays	1330	9.7	Cynwyl Elfed	1549	57.9
Creigiau/St. Fagans	720	17.6	Cynwyl Gaeo	891	58.4
Cyncoed	1156	11.5	Dafen	1057	32.0
Ely	1342	9.6	Elli	1073	35.1
Fairwater	1090	9.2	Felinfoel	631	33.5
Gabalfa	811	10.9	Garnant	1331	69.6
Grangetown	1221	8.9	Glanamman	1476	67.1
Heath	1327	11.7	Glanymor	1153	24.5
Lisvane	339	10.5	Glyn	1297	65.8
Llandaff	1329	15.2	Gorslas	2551	70.4
Llandaff North	864	10.9	Hendy	1528	52.1
Llanishen	1688	11.0	Hengoed	1407	37.9

	Welsh-speakers			Welsh-speakers	
	No.	%		No.	%

Kidwelly	1614	50.7	Aberteifi/Cardigan -		
Laugharne Township	681	23.8	Teifi	581	50.4
Llanboidy	1050	54.4	Aberystwyth Bronglais	817	42.9
Llanddarog	1122	63.1	Aberystwyth Canol/		
Llandeilo	1569	55.2	Central	614	28.6
Llandovery	1318	47.0	Aberystwyth Gogledd/		
Llandybie	2250	62.3	North	608	31.5
Llanegwad	1413	59.9	Aberystwyth Penparcau	1180	39.6
Llanfihangel Aberbythych	942	56.8	Aberystwyth Rheidol	836	34.8
Llanfihangel-ar-Arth	1750	66.4	Beulah	858	54.1
Llangadog	1139	60.0	Borth	927	42.6
Llangeler	1875	60.2	Capel Dewi	757	56.1
Llangennech	2021	46.4	Ceulanamaesmawr	1048	56.3
Llangunnor	1196	54.0	Ciliau Aeron	1140	58.4
Llangyndeyrn	1865	65.4	Faenor	926	39.2
Llannon	3440	71.1	Lampeter	1443	51.5
Llansteffan	1051	49.0	Llanarth	854	56.8
Llanybydder	1583	64.5	Llanbadarn Fawr - Padarn	499	40.4
Lliedi	1592	32.7	Llanbadarn Fawr - Sulien	377	23.5
Llwynhendy	1356	33.0	Llandyfriog	1036	58.5
Manordeilo and Salem	1015	49.4	Llandysiliogogo	988	51.8
Pembrey	1320	36.4	Llandysul Town	1030	70.0
Penygroes	1643	70.0	Llanfarian	766	54.6
Pontamman	1520	60.1	Llanfihangel Ystrad	1251	62.9
Pontyberem	1992	73.3	Llangeitho	883	57.1
Quarter Bach	2129	74.9	Llangybi	934	54.6
Saron	2179	65.1	Llanrhystyd	897	62.4
St. Clears	1537	56.3	Llansantffraed	1335	55.0
St. Ishmael	1402	55.3	Llanwenog	1185	64.7
Swiss Valley	864	36.2	Lledrod	1287	59.3
Trelech	1243	60.8	Melindwr	1088	51.6
Trimsaran	1403	57.0	New Quay	507	46.7
Tycroes	1208	58.1	Penbryn	1063	52.1
Tyisha	1098	28.5	Pen-parc	1317	57.5
Whitland	904	45.2	Tirymynach	1088	59.9
			Trefeurig	928	57.5
Ceredigion			Tregaron	804	67.9
Aberaeron	950	64.2	Troedyraur	802	58.4
Aberporth	1189	48.9	Ystwyth	1150	59.2
Aberteifi/Cardigan -					
Mwldan	1059	62.5	**Conwy**		
Aberteifi/Cardigan -			Abergele Pensarn	292	13.9
Rhyd-y-Fuwch	770	64.2	Betws yn Rhos	868	46.2

151

	Welsh-speakers			Welsh-speakers	
	No.	%		No.	%
Betws-y-Coed	645	55.8	Dyserth	508	20.6
Bryn	878	45.7	Efenechtyd	821	51.6
Caerhun	817	44.4	Llanarmon-yn-Ial/		
Capelulo	525	37.0	Llandegla	555	25.4
Colwyn	933	22.6	Llanbedr Dyffryn Clwyd/		
Conwy	1313	33.2	Llangynhafal	512	33.9
Craig-y-Don	696	20.9	Llandrillo	701	64.4
Crwst	1166	63.2	Llandyrnog	832	41.3
Deganwy	835	23.2	Llanfair Dyffryn Clwyd/		
Eglwysbach	786	54.1	Gwyddelwern	1167	53.4
Eirias	842	25.8	Llangollen	758	19.9
Gele	994	23.1	Llanrhaeadr-yng-		
Glyn	847	22.1	Nghinmeirch	1085	59.0
Gogarth	645	18.4	Prestatyn Central	634	18.2
Gower	710	66.1	Prestatyn East	746	17.7
Kinmel Bay	584	10.8	Prestatyn Meliden	405	19.4
Llanddulas	352	23.1	Prestatyn North	611	12.3
Llandrillo yn Rhos	1236	17.8	Prestatyn South West	396	12.5
Llangernyw	895	69.3	Rhuddlan	888	21.4
Llansanffraid	790	35.5	Rhyl East	601	13.5
Llansannan	1161	65.5	Rhyl South	618	17.6
Llysfaen	591	23.5	Rhyl South East	1127	16.1
Marl	1095	30.3	Rhyl South West	755	15.3
Mochdre	434	24.2	Rhyl West	506	12.4
Mostyn	680	19.7	Ruthin	2172	42.9
Pandy	950	55.3	St. Asaph East	439	25.5
Pant-yr-afon/Penmaenan	877	37.9	St. Asaph West	382	23.4
Penrhyn	1011	21.8	Trefnant	587	32.6
Pensarn	860	33.1	Tremeirchion	473	30.6
Pentre Mawr	722	21.6			
Rhiw	989	17.6	**Flintshire**		
Towyn	230	10.5	Argoed	418	14.9
Trefriw	648	50.0	Aston	320	9.8
Tudno	1173	25.5	Bagillt East	229	12.7
Uwch Conwy	968	66.8	Bagillt West	275	14.0
Uwchaled	1004	73.6	Broughton North East	187	9.3
			Broughton South	345	9.7
Denbighshire			Brynford	402	18.4
Bodelwyddan	366	18.1	Buckley Bistre East	314	9.3
Corwen	1197	51.4	Buckley Bistre West	456	10.5
Denbigh Central	708	36.7	Buckley Mountain	262	10.9
Denbigh Lower	1896	44.3	Buckley Pentrobin	378	9.6
Denbigh Upper/Henllan	1094	36.3	Caergwrle	194	12.1

	No.	%
Caerwys	576	23.6
Cilcain	349	19.1
Connah's Quay Central	315	10.1
Connah's Quay Golftyn	674	12.9
Connah's Quay South	660	12.1
Connah's Quay Wepre	227	11.0
Ewloe	564	12.1
Ffynnongroyw	544	25.7
Flint Castle	277	13.4
Flint Coleshill	541	14.0
Flint Oakenholt	368	13.2
Flint Trelawny	484	13.7
Greenfield	364	13.8
Gronant	233	15.1
Gwernaffield	320	17.7
Gwernymynydd	361	20.9
Halkyn	385	23.1
Hawarden	148	8.1
Higher Kinnerton	172	10.9
Holywell Central	248	14.0
Holywell East	304	17.2
Holywell West	421	18.9
Hope	319	13.1
Leeswood	325	15.7
Llanfynydd	308	18.1
Mancot	361	10.8
Mold Broncoed	456	18.8
Mold East	308	16.3
Mold South	775	29.0
Mold West	355	15.7
Mostyn	385	19.9
New Brighton	389	13.4
Northop	454	15.7
Northop Hall	206	12.8
Penyffordd	463	12.9
Queensferry	179	9.7
Saltney Mold Junction	126	9.7
Saltney Stonebridge	291	8.9
Sealand	229	8.7
Shotton East	209	12.0
Shotton Higher	252	10.4
Shotton West	148	8.0

	No.	%
Trelawnyd and Gwaenysgor	500	27.0
Treuddyn	407	26.8
Whitford	467	21.4
Gwynedd		
Aberdaron	743	75.1
Aberdovey	464	41.9
Abererch	1073	76.8
Abermaw	1021	43.5
Abersoch	439	50.2
Arllechwedd	812	60.8
Bala	1530	79.7
Bethel	1157	86.0
Bontnewydd	944	84.4
Botwnnog	714	77.1
Bowydd and Rhiw	1398	79.4
Brithdir/Llanfachreth/ Ganllwyd/Llanelltyd	901	66.0
Bryn-crug/Llanfihangel	583	58.1
Cadnant	1751	85.5
Clynnog	556	67.5
Corris/Mawddwy	707	60.4
Criccieth	1152	65.1
Cwm-y-Glo	648	72.5
Deiniol	404	30.4
Deiniolen	1270	75.6
Dewi	870	58.9
Diffwys and Maenofferen	902	83.7
Dolbenmaen	799	69.7
Dolgellau North	791	67.0
Dolgellau South	1027	73.0
Dyffryn Ardudwy	783	48.4
Efail-Newydd/Buan	937	76.4
Garth	456	46.0
Gerlan	1592	74.3
Glyder	957	54.9
Groeslon	1265	80.3
Harlech	1105	58.8
Hendre	707	51.9
Hirael	692	52.7
Llanaelhaearn	1173	77.6

	Welsh-speakers			Welsh-speakers	
	No.	%		No.	%

Llanbedr	496	50.2	Gurnos	326	6.8
Llanbedrog	521	52.2	Merthyr Vale	394	10.4
Llanberis	1559	80.0	Park	386	9.2
Llandderfel	1034	72.3	Penydarren	417	8.2
Llanengan	710	65.4	Plymouth	456	9.4
Llangelynin	800	40.7	Town	666	10.5
Llanllyfni	860	74.0	Treharris	688	11.4
Llanrug	1500	86.6	Vaynor	360	10.8
Llanuwchllyn	653	80.7			
Llanwnda	1493	82.2	**Monmouthshire**		
Llanystumdwy	1439	77.3	Caerwent	132	8.0
Marchog	1388	54.1	Caldicot Castle	254	10.8
Menai (Bangor)	692	27.4	Cantref	325	10.9
Menai (Caernarfon)	1741	83.7	Castle	42	9.0
Morfa Nefyn	954	77.1	Croesonen	144	9.4
Nefyn	1031	78.5	Crucorney	162	8.6
Ogwen	1723	79.0	Devauden	92	6.9
Peblig (Caernarfon)	1942	88.0	Dewstow	135	9.4
Penisarwaun	1230	74.1	Dixton with Osbaston	103	7.0
Penrhyndeudraeth	1823	76.7	Drybridge	192	6.5
Pentir	1436	62.1	Goetre Fawr	233	10.3
Penygroes	1479	87.9	Green Lane	107	12.8
Porthmadog East	1396	84.3	Grofield	141	8.3
Porthmadog West	1138	64.8	Lansdown	129	8.3
Porthmadog-Tremadog	940	69.4	Larkfield	124	9.5
Pwllheli North	1491	81.5	Llanbadoc	118	9.0
Pwllheli South	1492	78.4	Llanelly Hill	349	9.4
Seiont	2518	87.2	Llanfoist Fawr	157	9.7
Talysarn	1227	71.5	Llangybi Fawr	123	7.4
Teigl	1454	80.0	Llanover	183	8.3
Trawsfynydd	1128	76.2	Llantilio Crossenny	102	6.5
Tregarth &			Llanwenarth Ultra	115	8.7
Mynydd Llandygai	1486	69.2	Mardy	223	9.7
Tudweiliog	585	74.1	Mill	432	9.9
Tywyn	1270	40.5	Mitchel Troy	81	7.1
Waunfawr	1102	72.8	Overmonnow	158	7.1
Y Felinheli	1441	71.9	Portskewett	230	11.6
			Priory	229	8.6
Merthyr Tydfil			Raglan	126	7.5
Bedlinog	290	8.8	Rogiet	179	11.7
Cyfarthfa	771	13.0	Severn	348	10.9
Dowlais	674	10.5	Shirenewton	166	8.5

	Welsh-speakers			Welsh-speakers	
	No.	%		No.	%
St. Arvans	137	9.8	Pontardawe	1818	37.2
St. Christopher's	193	10.6	Port Talbot	526	10.3
St. Kingsmark	185	7.5	Resolven	381	12.6
St. Mary's	108	6.4	Rhos	690	28.5
The Elms	139	9.7	Sandfields East	472	7.9
Thornwell	396	12.5	Sandfields West	568	8.8
Trellech United	153	6.5	Seven Sisters	500	25.5
Usk	171	7.6	Tai-bach	335	7.6
West End	143	9.2	Tonna	322	13.4
Wyesham	168	8.4	Trebanos	575	42.0
			Ystalyfera	1604	54.2
Neath/Port Talbot					
Aberavon	396	7.7	**Newport**		
Aberdulais	303	16.1	Allt-yr-yn	759	9.2
Allt-wen	793	35.6	Alway	899	11.1
Baglan	669	10.3	Beechwood	647	8.8
Blaengwrach	297	15.4	Bettws	773	9.7
Briton Ferry East	279	10.0	Caerleon	851	10.0
Briton Ferry West	256	9.3	Gaer	781	9.5
Bryn and Cwmavon	1250	19.8	Graig	562	10.6
Bryn-coch North	355	16.0	Langstone	268	7.1
Bryn-coch South	697	13.8	Liswerry	929	9.1
Cadoxton	248	15.9	Llanwern	304	10.4
Cimla	452	11.1	Malpas	797	10.2
Coedffranc Central	453	12.0	Marshfield	384	9.4
Coedffranc North	299	13.2	Pillgwenlly	473	9.3
Coedffranc West	238	11.9	Ringland	658	8.1
Crynant	543	29.6	Rogerstone	855	10.0
Cwmllynfell	742	68.2	Shaftesbury	521	9.9
Cymmer	219	7.8	St. Julians	845	10.1
Dyffryn	351	11.4	Stow Hill	364	8.5
Glyncorrwg	100	8.9	Tredegar Park	402	12.6
Glynneath	786	22.9	Victoria	536	8.4
Godre'r graig	577	41.3			
Gwaun-Cae-Gurwen	1853	67.7	**Pembrokeshire**		
Gwynfi	116	8.1	Amroth	139	11.5
Lower Brynamman	857	67.8	Burton	171	11.8
Margam	249	10.8	Camrose	386	17.0
Neath East	599	10.4	Carew	160	11.9
Neath North	452	12.0	Cilgerran	972	52.4
Neath South	470	10.5	Clydau	796	57.5
Onllwyn	247	21.0	Crymych	1421	63.4
Pelenna	245	21.5	Dinas Cross	808	54.2

| | Welsh-speakers | | | Welsh-speakers | |
	No.	%			No.	%
East Williamston	249	11.0		Pembroke:		
Fishguard North East	636	38.3		St. Michael	250	11.9
Fishguard North West	584	41.2		Penally	196	12.7
Goodwick	551	30.9		Rudbaxton	311	19.5
Haverfordwest: Castle	300	15.8		Saundersfoot	290	10.7
Haverfordwest: Garth	371	14.4		Scleddau	512	38.9
Haverfordwest: Portfield	344	16.2		Solva	469	34.0
Haverfordwest:				St. David's	629	36.0
Prendergast	312	18.3		St. Dogmaels	1063	51.1
Haverfordwest: Priory	325	15.8		St. Ishmael's	181	13.1
Hundleton	198	12.3		Tenby: North	254	12.1
Johnston	294	13.6		Tenby: South	280	10.5
Kilgetty/Begelly	218	11.3		The Havens	200	15.5
Lampeter Velfrey	346	24.5		Wiston	433	26.1
Lamphey	182	11.9				
Letterston	846	42.6		**Powys**		
Llangwm	255	13.3		Aber-craf	625	45.7
Llanrhian	697	49.5		Banwy	542	60.2
Maenclochog	1523	55.2		Beguildy	181	12.9
Manorbier	237	12.7		Berriew	174	13.7
Martletwy	238	18.5		Blaen Hafren	570	27.6
Merlin's Bridge	353	17.1		Bronllys	132	11.1
Milford: Central	181	10.0		Builth	367	16.1
Milford: East	219	11.3		Bwlch	87	9.8
Milford: Hakin	228	10.2		Caersws	600	28.4
Milford: Hubberston	307	13.4		Churchstoke	109	7.2
Milford: North	294	13.4		Crickhowell	272	10.1
Milford: West	239	11.5		Cwm-twrch	1003	54.6
Narberth	432	23.9		Disserth and Trecoed	143	12.6
Narberth Rural	242	19.3		Dolforwyn	227	14.2
Newport	529	48.6		Felin-fâch	170	14.2
Neyland: East	231	11.1		Forden	170	13.4
Neyland: West	233	12.0		Glantwymyn	1137	60.2
Pembroke Dock: Central	161	10.9		Glasbury	194	9.6
Pembroke Dock: Llanion	301	12.3		Guilsfield	334	16.1
Pembroke Dock: Market	199	12.8		Gwernyfed	127	8.7
Pembroke Dock: Pennar	352	12.3		Hay	107	7.5
Pembroke: Monkton	190	11.8		Kerry	215	11.6
Pembroke:				Knighton	332	11.3
St. Mary North	232	12.4		Llanafanfawr	176	12.8
Pembroke:				Llanbadarn Fawr	129	12.6
St. Mary South	136	10.0		Llanbrynmair	502	53.8

	Welsh-speakers	
	No.	%
Llandinam	226	16.4
Llandrindod East/		
Llandrindod West	124	11.2
Llandrindod North	245	13.9
Llandrindod South	233	11.7
Llandrinio	222	13.1
Llandysilio	165	10.9
Llanelwedd	119	10.8
Llanfair Caereinion	602	38.5
Llanfihangel	545	53.0
Llanfyllin	540	39.4
Llangattock	96	9.7
Llangors	143	14.0
Llangunllo	118	9.8
Llangynidr	137	14.0
Llanidloes	485	17.8
Llanrhaeadr-ym-		
Mochnant	783	54.6
Llanrhaeadr-ym-		
Mochnant/Llansilin	685	39.6
Llansantffraid	354	21.1
Llanwrtyd Wells	378	22.4
Llanyre	138	13.4
Machynlleth	1124	54.2
Maescar/Llywel	496	28.4
Meifod	315	24.7
Montgomery	140	11.5
Nantmel	189	13.2
Newtown Central	494	16.1
Newtown East	269	14.1
Newtown		
Llanllwchaiarn North	308	16.4
Newtown		
Llanllwchaiarn West	279	16.6
Newtown South	205	11.6
Old Radnor	149	9.7
Presteigne	250	10.4
Rhayader	302	15.0
Rhiwcynon	415	23.0
St. David Within	201	12.5
St. John	542	16.6
St. Mary	366	13.3
Talgarth	167	10.5

	Welsh-speakers	
	No.	%
Talybont-on-Usk	265	14.4
Tawe-Uchaf	619	30.8
Trewern	116	10.4
Welshpool Castle	194	13.0
Welshpool Gungrog	343	13.8
Welshpool Llanerchyddol	301	14.7
Ynyscedwyn	1119	52.7
Yscir	200	18.6
Ystradgynlais	1185	47.8

Rhondda Cynon Taf

	Welsh-speakers	
	No.	%
Aberaman North	468	9.5
Aberaman South	452	9.9
Abercynon	518	8.3
Aberdare East	827	13.2
Aberdare West/		
Llwydcoed	1281	14.2
Beddau	540	12.5
Brynna	479	13.5
Church Village	445	14.0
Cilfynydd	378	13.8
Cwm Clydach	250	8.2
Cwmbach	495	12.0
Cymmer	544	9.5
Ferndale	546	12.7
Gilfach Goch	287	8.7
Glyncoch	343	12.2
Graig	287	12.1
Hawthorn	376	10.5
Hirwaun	710	18.4
Llanharan	430	13.1
Llanharry	346	12.4
Llantrisant Town	709	17.4
Llantwit Fardre	890	14.9
Llwyn-y-pia	188	8.6
Maerdy	353	10.6
Mountain Ash East	277	10.5
Mountain Ash West	442	10.6
Penrhiwceiber	505	8.4
Pentre	609	11.6
Pen-y-graig	482	8.5
Pen-y-waun	348	11.0
Pont-y-clun	803	14.5

	Welsh-speakers No.	%		Welsh-speakers No.	%
Pontypridd Town	550	19.3	Morriston	2397	14.8
Porth	728	12.7	Mynyddbach	994	11.7
Rhigos	298	17.7	Newton	360	11.7
Rhondda	584	12.9	Oystermouth	421	10.0
Rhydfelen Central/Ilan	588	13.2	Penclawdd	640	18.0
Taffs Well	556	16.1	Penderry	786	7.5
Talbot Green	301	12.6	Penllergaer	440	18.8
Ton-teg	604	13.9	Pennard	257	9.9
Tonypandy	339	10.1	Penyrheol	991	17.7
Tonyrefail East	665	11.9	Pontardulais	1956	38.2
Tonyrefail West	506	10.1	Sketty	1527	11.3
Trallwng	503	13.1	St. Thomas	392	6.4
Trealaw	316	8.4	Townhill	552	6.8
Treforest	459	9.2	Uplands	1494	11.4
Treherbert	875	15.1	Upper Loughor	610	22.1
Treorchy	1250	15.9	West Cross	584	9.2
Tylorstown	514	11.3			
Tyn-y-nant	457	12.6	**Torfaen**		
Ynyshir	407	12.2	Abersychan	786	11.9
Ynysybwl	651	14.1	Blaenavon	539	9.6
Ystrad	746	12.3	Brynwern	139	8.0
			Coed Eva	283	12.3
Swansea			Croesyceiliog North	345	10.3
Bishopston	321	9.9	Croesyceiliog South	179	10.0
Bonymaen	636	10.4	Cwmyniscoy	133	10.6
Castle	1030	8.8	Fairwater	724	13.5
Clydach	1672	23.7	Greenmeadow	524	12.3
Cockett	1434	11.8	Llantarnam	426	9.3
Cwmbwrla	738	9.3	Llanyrafon North	223	11.4
Dunvant	449	9.9	Llanyrafon South	289	11.1
Fairwood	330	12.2	New Inn	597	9.7
Gorseinon	552	17.6	Panteg	662	9.9
Gower	369	10.4	Pontnewydd	593	10.0
Gowerton	739	15.5	Pontnewynydd	164	11.0
Killay North	322	9.6	Pontypool	128	7.7
Killay South	213	9.5	Snatchwood	173	9.4
Kingsbridge	849	21.4	St. Cadocs and Penygarn	149	9.6
Landore	481	8.2	St. Dials	403	11.0
Llangyfelach	847	20.1	Trevethin	404	11.5
Llansamlet	1713	14.9	Two Locks	714	11.4
Lower Loughor	388	18.7	Upper Cwmbran	612	11.2
Mawr	792	45.3	Wainfelin	236	10.1
Mayals	305	11.0			

	Welsh-speakers			Welsh-speakers	
	No.	%		No.	%
Vale of Glamorgan			Grosvenor	275	12.1
Baruc	709	12.7	Gwenfro	231	13.3
Buttrills	655	11.3	Gwersyllt East and South	415	9.9
Cadoc	772	9.8	Gwersyllt North	256	10.2
Castleland	347	9.9	Gwersyllt West	347	11.8
Cornerswell	528	10.0	Hermitage	291	12.9
Court	489	10.6	Holt	255	9.3
Cowbridge	792	12.8	Johnstown	696	21.4
Dinas Powys	801	10.3	Little Acton	304	13.2
Dyfan	539	11.0	Llangollen Rural	331	17.1
Gibbonsdown	596	10.8	Llay	488	10.3
Illtyd	885	11.0	Maesydre	252	13.0
Llandough	167	8.9	Marchwiel	266	11.3
Llandow/Ewenny	325	12.9	Marford and Hoseley	232	9.8
Llantwit Major	1236	11.9	Minera	491	20.9
Peterston-super-Ely	265	12.1	New Broughton	298	9.8
Plymouth	579	11.7	Offa	273	12.9
Rhoose	604	11.2	Overton	302	9.9
St. Athan	341	9.3	Pant	696	32.0
St. Augustine's	598	10.8	Penycae	453	21.0
St. Bride's Major	299	11.3	Penycae and		
Stanwell	488	12.3	Ruabon South	405	17.9
Sully	432	10.5	Plas Madoc	244	14.0
Wenvoe	287	10.6	Ponciau	1626	37.4
			Queensway	225	9.7
Wrexham			Rhosnesni	342	11.6
Acton	334	11.4	Rossett	243	7.6
Borras Park	286	11.7	Ruabon	317	13.7
Bronington	314	10.0	Smithfield	195	9.5
Brymbo	404	15.8	Stansty	242	11.4
Bryn Cefn	229	12.2	Whitegate	289	10.9
Brynyffynnon	386	12.9	Wynnstay	195	9.3
Cartrefle	207	9.4			
Cefn	667	14.2	**Ynys Môn**		
Chirk North	291	12.0	Aberffraw	876	69.3
Chirk South	205	11.3	Amlwch Port	906	67.3
Coedpoeth	956	21.1	Amlwch Rural	678	56.4
Dyffryn Ceiriog/			Beaumaris	788	39.6
Ceiriog Valley	769	34.3	Bodffordd	1155	77.5
Erddig	387	17.9	Bodorgan	1084	72.2
Esclusham	373	14.4	Braint	1110	76.9
Garden Village	301	14.9	Bryngwran	1233	76.0
Gresford East and West	311	11.1	Brynteg	900	50.7

	Welsh–speakers	
	No.	**%**
Cadnant	535	51.4
Cefni	1146	82.7
Cwm Cadnant	1218	55.9
Cyngar	1413	84.0
Gwyngyll	1117	73.8
Holyhead Town	443	42.5
Kingsland	655	47.7
Llanbadrig	733	54.1
Llanbedrgoch	709	45.5
Llanddyfnan	876	69.5
Llaneilian	1333	61.3
Llanfaethlu	1017	66.8
Llanfair-yn-Neubwll	1336	51.3
Llanfihangel Ysgeifiog	1519	77.8
Llangoed	674	54.4
Llanidan	1107	68.5
Llannerch-y-medd	1246	71.9
London Road	737	51.4
Maeshyfryd	929	43.5
Mechell	946	63.8
Moelfre	560	51.1
Morawelon	667	44.7
Parc a'r Mynydd	589	53.2
Pentraeth	1005	58.1
Porthyfelin	1011	45.4
Rhosneigr	405	42.5
Rhosyr	1333	63.4
Trearddur	975	42.4
Tudur	1185	83.3
Tysilio	1282	64.3
Valley	1278	54.8